Between Dying and Not Dying, I Chose the Guitar

The Pandemic Years in New Orleans

http://ulpress.org
University of Louisiana at Lafayette Press
P.O. Box 43558
Lafayette, LA 70504-3558

Printed in the United States

Library of Congress Cataloging-in-Publication Data

Names: Nolan, James, 1947- author. | Codrescu, Andrei, 1946- writer of forward.
Title: Between dying and not dying, I chose the guitar : the pandemic years in New Orleans / James Nolan ; foreword by Andrei Codrescu.
Description: Lafayette, LA : University of Louisiana at Lafayette Press, 2024.
Identifiers: LCCN 2023045679 | ISBN 9781959569084 (paperback)
Subjects: LCSH: Nolan, James, 1947- | Authors, American--Biography. | COVID-19 Pandemic, 2020---Personal narratives. | New Orleans (La.)--Biography
Classification: LCC PS3564.O36 Z46 2024 | DDC 813.54 [B]--dc23/eng/20231226
LC record available at https://lccn.loc.gov/2023045679

Cover art by Marsha Ercegovic
Cover design by Kathleen Grieshaber

Between Dying and Not Dying, I Chose the Guitar

The Pandemic Years in New Orleans

JAMES NOLAN

Foreword by Andrei Codrescu

2025
University of Louisiana at Lafayette Press

Also by James Nolan

Fiction

You Don't Know Me: New and Selected Stories (University of
Louisiana at Lafayette Press)
Higher Ground (University of Louisiana at Lafayette Press)
Perpetual Care: Stories (Jefferson Press)

Memoir

Flight Risk: Memoirs of a New Orleans Bad Boy (University Press
of Mississippi)

Poetry

Nasty Water: Collected New Orleans Poems (University of
Louisiana at Lafayette Press)
Drunk on Salt (Willow Springs Editions)
Why I Live in the Forest (Wesleyan University Press)
What Moves Is Not the Wind (Wesleyan University Press)

Poetry in Translation

Pablo Neruda, *Stones of the Sky* (Copper Canyon Press)
Jaime Gil de Biedma, *Longing: Selected Poems* (City Lights Books)

Criticism

*Poet-Chief: The Native American Poetics of Walt Whitman
and Pablo Neruda* (University of New Mexico Press)

Essays

*Fumadores en manos de un dios enfurecido: Ensayos
al caballo entre varios mundos* (Madrid: Editores Enigma)

In memory of those guiding lights of my life, the older artist friends who passed away while this book was being written: the writers and publishers Lawrence Ferlinghetti of City Lights and Richard Burgin of *Boulevard* magazine; writer Lee Meitzen Grue; painter JoAnna Coté; Joe DeSalvo of Faulkner House Books; Jazz Festival photographer Kichea Burt; printmaker Warrington Colescott, a fellow Creole whose art appears on the covers of two of my books; artist Jeanne Meinke; writer and former Barcelona City Council member Xavier Muñoz; and Spanish translator Pilar Vázquez of Madrid.

What do I have that I haven't been given?

Between dying and not dying,
I chose the guitar.

—Pablo Neruda, "Autumn Testament"

Contents

Francisco Goya, *Saturno devorando a su hijo* (Museo del Prado)

FOREWORD BY ANDREI CODRESCU

What Did We Do to Deserve This?

James Nolan is a lucky man. He was born after World War II, when history gave humans its longest break: seven decades. This was not a reward for suffering, not the sudden pity of a benevolent god, nor the anthropomorphized mercy of the machinery of the universe. Death was tired and full. As in the gruesome Goya painting, "Saturn Devouring His Son," it had eaten so many millions of its children in horrendously painful ways that its stomach hurt. It had to sleep, pass out, and repair itself. Death went in the shop to get its gears oiled, which it did during the seventy years Nolan and I believed that we had some kind of personal relationship with it.

Nolan, a *pur sang* New Orleanian, partakes in generations of the baroque worship of death. The graves of his ancestors, the moon over their cemeteries, the ghosts and vampires—both real and fake—inhabit his sense of place with the reanimating power of poetry. The dead rise in his stories refilled with the life they may or may not have had and the history their tombstones cannot tell. Because he was lucky enough to live a life of adventure and beauty, Nolan is capable of giving voice to the tombstones.

What is more, Nolan had a double serving of luck while death was in the shop. He was part of a generation permitted the luxury of an optimism not shared during our parents' era: my mother is a Holocaust survivor; his father liberated Nazi concentration camps. Our own optimism is a license to dream other worlds, to enter the lives of people born in the freedom of the imagination, to travel and return. As the Who sing when "talkin' about my g-g-g generation," boomers such as Nolan and I became outsiders by choice, an identity that only poets had claimed in the past, at a great cost to their health and lives. Among those rare creatures, the Romantic poets still live in schoolbooks, perennial models for ecstasy and its worth in misery.

We had time for a whole romantic generation to live and imagine everything, from nostalgia for past worlds to utopias in ages to come. In the United States death did take itself out for exercise and tests, especially at the height of the AIDS epidemic, but it still left enough of us the time to play and experience an exceptionally rare feeling of joy. We wrestled with that liberty through disobedience. We had the time to defy authority, to not obey rules: death was in the shop and might never recover.

Death was dead.

Right.

This journal of the plague years beginning in 2020, *Between Dying and Not Dying, I Chose the Guitar,* declares itself crisply on the side of poetry. Nolan chooses to disregard the border between death and life as an authoritarian trick of mind control. Even as he documents, with the flair of the great storyteller he is, the details of his life in a city where the life-loving citizens have been sentenced to solitary confinement, he finds the courage and humor to survive. It helps that the city is New Orleans and that his dead are across the street resurrected by his mind whenever the unbearable makes life too prosaic to live.

The mix of prescience, sobriety, satire, and curiosity that are the trademarks of James Nolan's writing shine here. The reader will discover them here as I have and will be amazed by the prophetic asides that have proven true after he finished writing the book, such the Queen of England's recent COVID-19 infection and the unleashing of war, that second Horseman of the Apocalypse, in the Russian invasion of Ukraine. James Nolan had the good "luck" as well (this one in quotes) of having lived in Communist China, Fascist Spain, and Colombia under a state of siege. The parallels between our recently mandated "good" behavior and the "good" behavior of people who live under such authoritarian regimes are unmistakable. Trump's America is no slouch when it comes to control, but his peculiar mix of circus, fraud, and conman chicanery frame this book as a uniquely American saga.

I have no doubt that Between *Dying and Not Dying, I Chose the Guitar* will take its place alongside Pepys, Defoe, and Camus among the great plague chronicles. Cited often by Nolan, with timeless affinity these writers will soothe forever the victims of pandemics to come.

Andrei Codrescu has written poetry, novels, and essays. He edited *Exquisite Corpse: A Journal of Books & Ideas*, was a senior commentator for National Public Radio, a chaired professor at LSU, and is a veteran of Katrina in New Orleans and the collapse of communism in his native Romania.

A Rough Draft of History

"This is what happened during the sickness."
—Thucydides, *History of the Peloponnesian War*

Like Sophocles, Boccaccio, Daniel Defoe, Samuel Pepys, Edgar Allan Poe, Albert Camus, Thomas Mann, William Burroughs, Tony Kushner, and other writers who have approached the subject of plagues, I'm an artist, not a scientist or politician. When dealing with a story of pestilence, either as an immediate threat or a metaphor for menace, I turn toward my imagination to shape it rather than to laboratories or public health policies. Those in power will write the definitive narrative of the coronavirus pandemic. And as a writer adrift during these saturnine years of 2020, 2021, and 2022, now staring out of my window at an alley in the Marigny neighborhood of New Orleans, I must emphasize the obvious: I'm not powerful. Nor am I in any position to speculate whether history, that final version of eventful times told by writers bestowed with authority, will match my personal story.

But I feel this is one worth telling.

Even as a southern fiction writer, poet, and memoirist, one with a grotesque and satiric edge to his aesthetic, I could never have made up the events of the past two years, beginning on the first day of lockdown in 2020, when my thriving life was abruptly canceled. I could never have foreseen the confusing and often contradictory public health policies, the divisive politics of the epidemic, or the smoldering civil war about vaccines and face masks. Nor could I have invented the ghostly Luling Mansion where I was living during much of this time, adjacent to the cemetery where four generations of my Creole family lie buried near Bayou St. John.

Neither could I have imagined how, at that very moment, the crew of an Amazon vampire movie shoot would arrive to paint the second-story walls of that phantasmal palazzo in the plague color palette—purple and scarlet—then disappear under strict health mandates, only to return months later to construct a Potemkin graveyard of the undead across the street, even as the coronavirus was ravaging the world. I could never have foreseen my eviction, mid-pandemic, during which I was forced to translate my household into a pyramid of boxes to move into this townhouse apartment on—of all places— Bourbon Street. Nor could I have dreamed up the loneliest New Year's Eve ever, or the Mardi-Gras-that-wasn't. Or my desperate search for a vaccine to keep this older man with a heart condition from dying.

I wish that I could have concocted such a plot for a thrilling new novel of the horror, dystopian, or speculative genres, but I didn't.

Because I was the protagonist, the plot was real enough, and it was happening to me.

The infectious disease epidemiologist Philip Alcabes writes that as a professor, "for years, I have occasionally offered a college course on epidemic narratives. Earlier versions of the course featured accounts of outbreaks by journalists, memoirists, novelists, playwrights, and screenwriters—that is, epidemics as shaped by one sensibility."

This is such a book.

As you'll discover in these pages, I'm a veteran of disruptive times, both of the medical and political varieties. "What's past is prologue," as Shakespeare cautions us in *The Tempest*. This is the third epidemic I've survived: first polio as a boy in the fifties, then AIDS as a bisexual living in San Francisco and Barcelona during the eighties and nineties, and now the coronavirus, well into my seventies. In each of these eras, I've been a member of the target demographic of the pandemic. As of January 6 of this year, this is the second attempted coup d'état I've witnessed, and one of three socially restrictive regimes I've lived under, of both the totalitarian Right and Left: Fascist Spain, a state of siege in Colombia, and just after the Maoist Cultural Revolution in China.

So nothing should surprise me, either on the medical or political fronts.

But these past two years have challenged my faith in human nature, in American democracy, and in the reliability of science to cure all of our ills, much less to sort out the truth. This week a friend wrote to me referring to the pandemic in the past tense: what it *meant* to her. This was even as the Omicron variant from South Africa was spiking a fifth surge in the United States, where the death toll already has topped nine hundred thousand, the most recorded mortalities of any country in the world. And many European, Asian, Latin American, and African countries were opening up their lockdowns only to slam them shut again in unpredictable patterns that make my head spin.

Although I'm now vaccinated and have finally taken off my face mask, I'm still listening to the guitar of my imagination. I write these words in the past tense of memoir as well as in the present tense of journalism, what former *Washington Post* publisher Philip Graham called "the first rough draft of history." For the moment, during this unsettling time between pre- and post-pandemic life, history seems to be broken, and the powerful have yet to rush in to fill the gap with their official interpretations of what has happened, why, and how it could have been avoided. Contrarian and exasperated as these observations often might seem, I hope that you'll find my own narrative engaging, entertaining, and somehow meaningful to your own. This disruptive era happened to all of us, each in our own particular way, and the challenge now is to connect our stories, making sense of our suddenly altered lives.

The rest, as they say, is history.

February 1, 2022
New Orleans

PART I

The Closing

*"If you don't know where you're going,
any road will get you there."*

—Lewis Carroll

1

For the first time this month, I sit on my balcony watching wispy clouds stream across the midnight blue sky, and in spite of a late March wind, feel peace. Medical experts claim that because of my age and underlying heart condition I could die tomorrow of this new plague, gasping for breath between blue lips.

Yet a transcendent calm has claimed me.

Everything has stopped. On a dime. As Mose Allison sings, "Just as well the world ended / it wasn't working anyway." That geyser of unlimited possibilities, fueled by a pumped up economy of gushing petroleum, traffic jams, tourist masses, soaring jets, mega churches, mega stars strutting across festival stages, five-star restaurant raves, and blockbuster hits, has come to a screeching halt. Of all places, Los Angeles now has the best air quality in the world, the gray cap of pollution over Beijing has lifted, and in Venice fish are swimming in the canals. No pedestrians venture out or headlights flash through this sepulchral evening in the Faubourg St. John neighborhood where I live in downtown New Orleans. Crows caw overhead, a cat screeches, and something quacks in the backyard patio three stories below. I never noticed before, but my neighbor must have gotten a duck.

The coronavirus has arrived. This last day of March 2020, the United States is now the epicenter of the global pandemic, outpacing China, Italy, and Spain in diagnosed cases and deaths. Dense New York City has almost half of the cases in the country, and as of today 101 deaths have been recorded in insular New Orleans, with only 380,000 residents. This three-hundred-year-old city, which has withstood numerous wars, fires, pestilences, and hurricanes under the flags of three different nations, is now a ghost town. National newscasters have taken to broadcasting stock footage of deserted Bourbon Street to drive home the eeriness of the current lockdown in American cities.

Everything has stopped and tonight, for the first time in two weeks, I appreciate it. My mind doesn't whirl with plans about where to go or what to do next because I can't go anywhere or do anything. Listening to Paco de Lucía's flamenco guitar, I pour myself a glass of Rioja wine. The evening air is redolent with night-blooming jasmine, an early summer scent as haunting as the perfume of a long-lost love. A brisk breeze billows the marquisette curtains as March goes out like a lamb, this same month that rushed in shrieking like a Greek harpy on steroids. The earth needed to pause for this breath of fresh air, and so did all of us living here. What is tragic is that a global pandemic had to provide this hiatus, at least for those of us fortunate enough to still be breathing without a respirator.

Breathe in. Breathe out. It's almost April Fool's Day.

2

Yet this is no practical joke.

On Monday, March 16, 2020, in this Chinese Year of the Metal Rat, my life was canceled in one fell swoop. A curt email from a student informed me that the conference room where I teach Wednesday writing workshops in her Warehouse District condo building was closed to any social gatherings. Another email let me know that the public library where I was to give a paid talk that Saturday about point-of-view in fiction was shut down. My own point-of-view grew rancid as I waited an hour for a public bus to come rumbling by to take me to my downtown gym. I really needed a swim and a good sweat in the steam room to calm down. The driver told me that this bus, the "Walmart to Cemeteries" line, was now running on a reduced schedule. And once I finally arrived at the health club, it also was closed. I soon learned that all restaurants, bars, coffee shops, theaters, museums, and other "non-essential businesses" in the city had been shut down. The only exceptions were grocery stores and pharmacies. On my way back from the closed gym, I stopped at the neighborhood grocery, only to find the shelves bare of most staples. People were starting to hoard, especially toilet paper, as if that alone could wipe away the reek of mortality.

When I'd left the house, movie set designers were scurrying around on the second floor of the building where I live. Known as the Luling Mansion, it's a decadent Italian-style palazzo built by the wealthy German cotton merchant Florenz Luling in 1865, designated as a historic landmark but one in sore need of preservation and repair. Now divided into ten shabby apartments, only four of which are occupied, it looms like a gothic granite phantom over the St. Louis Cemetery Number Three next door and nearby Bayou St. John. The set designers had been busy painting the walls of the two empty second-floor apartments purple and scarlet. This was in preparation for the upcoming shoot of an Amazon vampire film called *Black as Night*, to be filmed that week in three consecutive dusk-to-dawn sessions. We few tenants were to be relocated to hotels. My plan was to pocket the hotel reimbursement, stay, and put up with the klieg-lit vampires downstairs.

When I arrived home from the closed gym and the bare grocery shelves, the movie sets were empty and the row of white studio trucks parked out front gone. The "no parking" signs the film crew had tied to the iron fence spikes were removed. The shoot had been canceled by the city health department.

I breathed an enormous sigh of relief. I wouldn't be living on the set of a vampire movie during what I was soon to find out was a global plague, one that had just started to kill people in New Orleans. Exhausted, I plunked down my gym bag and the few groceries I'd been able to scrounge onto the dining table in my living room and sat there to stare out of the third-floor window. In the moonlight, faint white glimmers of the above ground tombs were visible through a tangle of branches. Although I couldn't spot it through the grove of live oaks, my own tomb was in that cemetery, the one in which my mother is buried, along with four generations of our Creole family.

At seventy-two, I knew that one day in the not too distant future I would take my place among them in that little peaked house sealed with white plaster. When I go, just roll me off the balcony, I joked to friends, and into the Glaudot tomb. At the moment, I noted that I had no fever, dry cough, or shortness of breath and wasn't ready to be rolled off the balcony.

Not yet. That was day one of the plague in New Orleans.

3

The next afternoon I phoned a friend in San Francisco, where I'd lived for several decades, only to learn that the City (as we called it) was also in lockdown. Then I called the airline to cancel the flight to San Francisco that I'd been planning for the following month, partly to hang in a place I once called home but primarily to escape the booming Jazz Fest that takes place every year in late April at the race-track next door. My bedroom window faces the Acura stage, where this year the Who were scheduled to perform.

What do you do when a half million drunken tourists show up at your house? My plan has always been to escape elsewhere to visit with friends. Now everyone in town agreed that the eight-day festival would be postponed. Along with the canceled vampire movie, that was another huge relief. Regularly inundated as we are by masses of tourists, we locals have gotten picky about which festivals, parades, cultural shindigs, and raucous crowds we can tolerate. Is this for us, we ask ourselves, or exclusively for them? If I don't spot somebody I know within the first fifteen minutes, it's for them. As cities go, this is still an inbred town.

Two weeks previously, for the first time ever while in New Orleans, I woke up during Carnival with a dark premonition not to mask and dive into the swarming hordes in the French Quarter for Mardi Gras. Although I'd been reading reports in the *New York Times* about the Wuhan virus, I was only dimly aware of the looming pandemic. Yet that weekend several people either had been crushed by parade floats, tumbled headfirst from their perches on floats, or plunged off toppling balconies. The corpses of two construction workers were still dangling inside the ruins of the collapsed Hard Rock Hotel on Canal Street. This year Carnival felt cursed, foreshadowed by death. The city had changed, I was adapting, so I didn't go. That was when scientists now believe New Orleans was "seeded," as they call it, with the coronavirus by the million Carnival revelers, many from New York, who arrived by way of infectious airports, planes, and cruise ships, those perfectly sealed incubators of the disease.

"Lockdown." "Social distancing." "Self-quarantining." "Flattening the curve." "An abundance of caution." "Sanitizing." "Super-spreader."

On and on drone the politicians, public health officials, and broadcasters. The language around the plague is forming a thick crust of cant, a catechism of euphemisms that insulate us from their impact the more they're repeated. The circuitous tone reminds me of George W. Bush's term for torture, "enhanced interrogation," or Trump press secretary Kellyanne Conway's "alternative facts," a clumsy tap dance around the word "lie." As Doctor Rieux comments in Camus's *The Plague*, "All our problems spring from our failure to use plain, clean-cut language."

I immediately distrust the spin factor in any public phenomenon that changes names midstream. We're now rebranding the coronavirus as COVID-19, because, I suppose, a name attached to a number sounds scarier and more official and can't be confused with a brand of Mexican beer or a royal coronation. Although I understand the genus and species distinction between the two terms, with this shift in nomenclature a visceral connection to a memorable image—the corona or crown—is missing. As the old Baptist ladies during my childhood used to say, "She'll get her crown in heaven." Now we pray that she doesn't get a crown of virus spikes in her lungs.

General Honoré's gruff "stay at home" feels more compelling, especially now that we have no choice.

4

I've put together a plague reading list from my library. First is Edgar Allan Poe's "The Masque of the Red Death," which I find in volume two of my grandfather's musty 1903 edition of the collected works, a five volume set. It's the perfect lockdown text, and rereading it sends a shiver down my spine. In Poe's story, the ornate chambers where Prince Prospero's masked guests hide from the plague are purple and scarlet, the same colors the set decorators had painted the empty second-story apartments where the vampire movie was to be filmed this month. Within Prince Prospero's locked and sealed compound, "the external world could take care of itself. In the meantime, it was folly to grieve, or to think. . . . All those and security were within. Without was the 'Red Death.'"

On the landing of the staircase leading up to my third-story apartment stands a mute ebony grandfather clock, one that hasn't chimed for decades, if not a century. In Poe's story there also "stood against the Western wall a clock of ebony. Its pendulum swung to and fro with a dull, heavy, monotonous clang." When this ominous clock chimes the hour, the revelers cloistered with Prince Prospero from the Red Death halt their dancing and "the giddiest grew pale, and the more aged and sedate passed their hands over their brows as if in confused reverie or meditation. . . . And then, for a moment, all is still, and all is silent save the voice of the clock."

We know what they are listening for: the appointed hour of their own mortality. After the masked Red Death has snuck into the fortress and followed Prince Prospero into the final chamber, where he and his guests succumb to the plague, "the life of the ebony clock went out."

Now, every time I leave the building, I shudder as I pass the silent ebony clock on the staircase landing to walk through the abandoned purple and scarlet film set on the second floor.

In one of these apartments downstairs, rows of plaster death masks are mounted above the crown moldings of the eighteen-foot ceilings. The walls remain painted those alarming colors because the film crew plans to return here "when all this is over," although I suspect that Amazon will simply cut its losses and finish shooting *Black as Night* in a sound studio. Before the crew left, I insisted they return the foyer to its original ivory color. They had painted it a depressing shade of enamel gunmetal gray, which made entering the building feel as claustrophobic as walking into a submarine.

Next on my reading list is a 1960 Signet Classic edition of Daniel Defoe's *A Journal of the Plague Year*, a sixty-cent paperback I've been lugging around since college. It still has my dorm room number scrawled next to my name on the inside cover. The cover image, bordered in purple, is of a hooded woman in a scarlet face mask. That seems to be the plague color palette: purple and scarlet.

"Social distancing" reminds me of Defoe's portrait of the 1665 bubonic plague in London, during which everyone hid inside their houses, the streets were emptied, pubs were closed, public "feasting" banned, and nobody tolerated any outside personal contact.

Unfortunately, as we now know, the *yersinia pestis* that infected the lymph nodes of its victims until they swelled into blackened buboes was spread by bites from the fleas infesting black rats, not by person-to-person contagion. So holing up inside rat-infested houses was the worst prevention possible. To escape the city, many moved to boats on the Thames, where the holds were filled with rats. "Nobody would suffer a stranger to come near them," Defoe writes. "The strange temper of the people of London at that time contributed extremely to their own destruction."

To add to the misery, the authorities ordered the killing of all cats and dogs, which, of course, had kept the rat population at bay. Pages and pages of the novel are dedicated to quoting the numerous other municipal health edicts issued to prevent a collapse of the destabilized government, rules as confusing as the ones we receive now about wearing face masks or not, singing the "Happy Birthday" song twice while scrubbing our hands, bumping elbows instead of handshakes, or wiping down groceries.

An earlier European outbreak of the Black Death is described in Giovanni Boccaccio's *The Decameron*, a fourteenth-century Italian epic in which what we'd now call a "socially distanced pod" of ten young people sequester themselves inside a villa in Fiesole, a town near Florence. There they take turns spinning a hundred tales to avoid the ravages of the bubonic plague that in 1348 killed a hundred thousand people within the strictly quarantined Tuscan capital. In the narrative frame to the stories, Boccaccio writes that "touching the clothes of the sick or anything touched or used by them seemed to communicate this very disease to the person involved." To avoid this lethal contamination, people like these young fabulists "gathered in small groups and lived entirely apart from everyone else. They shut themselves up in those houses where there were no sick people," only, as we now suspect, rats crawling with fleas infected with *yersinia pestis*. On the other hand, in an aside that mirrors today's blithe lockdown resisters, Boccaccio notes that "others thought the opposite: they believed that drinking excessively, enjoying life, going about singing and celebrating . . . making light of everything that happened was the best medicine for the disease."

We Americans shouldn't feel so singular about our polarized pandemic politics: *plus ça change, plus c'est la même chose.*

Next on my plague reading list is a brittle paperback of the Kenneth Burke translation of Thomas Mann's *Death in Venice*, a novella that inspired my pilgrimage to Venice in the early seventies. There I sat on the Lido beach in front of the Grand Hôtel des Bains scanning the horizon for an apparition of the angelic adolescent boy Tadzio, imagining the haughty, middle-aged German writer Gustav von Aschenbach dying of the cholera epidemic as he takes a last lingering glance at the lost beauty of youth. Every time I hear the swelling Adagietto of Mahler's Fifth Symphony, I picture black hair dye dribbling down Dirk Bogarde's feverish face as his eyelids fold shut in the final beach scene of Visconti's film version.

Yet in this reading what captures my attention isn't the morbidly decadent eroticism that once attracted me to the book, but the firsthand account of a cholera outbreak that Mann witnessed during his journey through Italy in 1911. In a 1930 diary, he wrote that "nothing is invented in *Death in Venice.*" With by now familiar verisimilitude, as true today as it was then, he captures the hypocrisy of the city authorities in dissimulating the sudden appearance of a so-called "Asiatic" cholera. It's significant that Boccaccio also describes the Florentine plague as originating "some years earlier in the east," as if Asia were the menacing source of all infections, like Trump's Kung Flu. In contaminated Venice, nobody will tell Aschenbach the truth. At the time, nobody acknowledged that the disease was spread by water contaminated with human waste, as the first epidemiologist John Snow discovered in 1850, and symptoms of the epidemic were blamed on the sirocco winds and rotten shellfish, even as wealthy tourists fled amid the abrasive stench of germicide. Although last February the Carnival in Venice was canceled because of the coronavirus pandemic in neighboring Lombardy, at the same time the Carnival that brought the virus to New Orleans proceeded here full speed ahead because, as in Mann's novel, "the authorities were more actuated by fear of being out of pocket . . . or by the apprehension of the large loses the hotels and shops that catered to foreigners would suffer in case of panic and blockade. And the fears of the people supported the persistent official policy of silence and denial."

An English travel clerk finally explains to Aschenbach in excruciating detail the mortal dangers of the cholera epidemic descending upon the city, where the quarantined buildings and orphanages are filled with the dying. "Recoveries were rare. Eighty out of every hundred died, and horribly, for the onslaught was of the extremest violence, and not infrequently of the 'dry' type, the most malignant form of contagion." He warns the German that "You would do well . . . to leave today instead of tomorrow. The blockade cannot be more than a few days off." After which, in besotted denial, the failing writer marches out of the travel agency to visit a barber, where he has his hair dyed and lips rouged to further pursue the elusive young Tadzio. Just as most of us here, following the news of the burgeoning pandemic in New York, continued to design our Mardi Gras costumes. Even though I didn't participate in the ill-fated festivities this year, I heard that on Fat Tuesday more than a few papier-mâche headdresses shaped like the spiked globes of the coronavirus went parading through the streets.

Whether in fin de siècle Venice or twenty-first-century New Orleans, those who live by tourism die by tourism.

Although in the plague-ridden history of this port city, once known as "the Necropolis of the South," commercial indifference to public health hasn't always been the cause of our ongoing malaise. The authorities in New Orleans really didn't understand the origins of our most deadly contagion, the yellow fever epidemic of the nineteenth century, long believed to be spread by "miasmas" in the city's marshy terrain. Soldiers shot cannons to dispel the hot, humid swamp gas emanating from what one commentator in 1850 called "this boiling fountain of death . . . belching up its poison and malaria." Residents were advised to sleep on balconies and in courtyards to avoid contagion indoors, even though those were the perfect places to be bitten by female *Aedes aegypti* mosquitoes. It wasn't until 1900 that their bites were finally proven to transmit the virus, a theory that had been proposed but widely scorned twenty years earlier.

The fear, confusion, and superstition surrounding yellow fever are well portrayed in the little known *Toucoutou,*a novel published by Edward Larocque Tinker in 1928. This "tragic mulatto" story describes the effect of the epidemic on the life of a Creole of color able to *passe en blanc,* much as my great-grandmother Landry and her family did. Toucoutou's childhood French Quarter home is permeated with the "cardavric stench peculiar to yellow fever," in which Bujac, her infected French-born father, often spews "black vomit—like coffee grounds." A doctor treats the disease with the then cutting-edge techniques of leeches, mercurial purges, lit turpentine rags applied to bleed germs from scarified flesh, and "a freshly sliced onion by his bedside—they say it absorbs the sickness." He cautions Toucoutou's octoroon mother "be sure to change the slices often and burn them afterward or otherwise you will spread the disease. It is lucky for Bujac that he has it today when he can have the attention of an enlightened physician . . . . Rest assured that the latest discoveries of medical science are helping," meaning this scientist's trusty leeches and sliced onions. Although unaware that mosquitoes are spreading the infection, he at least understands the futility of burning tar and firing artillery to stop the epidemic. In an early plea for public health, the doctor insists that "if only they would clean up the stinking swamps that empest the city; if they would see to it that the filth from the cesspools is not washed into the houses on every flood, they might accomplish something." And that alone, of course, would have helped to control the swarms of mosquitoes spreading the illness.

During the late 1800s, 15 percent of the city's population fell to yellow fever, including four of my great-grandmother Landry's six siblings, who died in their home on Bourbon Street between June 29, 1882, and July 18, 1884. Their deaths occurred during what was known as the "sickly season," those summer months when mosquitoes breed. These family remains are buried deep inside our tomb next door, the one I can almost spot through the grove of live oaks. On the marble mantle next to the Landry clock, I keep a faded oval daguerreotype of one of Grande Mémère's brothers, Sylvère, who died in that epidemic, as seductive at fifteen as Tadzio was to Aschenbach, although with more exotic mulatto features. Understandably, my great-grandmother was a fanatic about keeping screen doors tightly closed. "Come back and close that screen door," she'd shout as this restless five-year-old scampered outside to play. "You'll let the mosquitoes in." Never for a moment did she let any standing water collect outside in which mosquito larvae could hatch.

During the fin de siècle, so pronounced was the fear of contagion in this "boiling fountain of death" that in 1894 New Orleans citizens threatened to burn to the ground what they called a "pest-house" at the corner of Perdido and Hagan Streets, one in which a dozen people lived who suffered from the ancient scourge of leprosy. A physician from the Tulane Medical School planned to found a leprosarium in the city, but widespread panic made that unthinkable, so this handful of patients was surreptitiously relocated to an abandoned plantation in Carville, a town along the Mississippi an hour northwest of the city. Ostensibly leased as an ostrich farm, Carville became the only sanatoriumin the United States dedicated to the care of those with Hansen's disease, although during more than a century of operation its peak population never reached more than four hundred. Patients were strictly quarantined there for the rest of their lives, and so great was the fear of contagion that even during a sensible era of recycling the glass Coke bottles from the sanatorium were not returnable. The patients chose alias names, under which they were buried, and anything they touched was burned. It wasn't until 2011 that armadillos were proven to be the originating source of Hansen's infection, and although person-to-person transmission of the disease does occur, it requires prolonged contact. Yet since Biblical times, so-called "lepers" were shunned and all contact avoided, because it was assumed that they left their deforming germs everywhere. And that the only leprosarium in the country would be founded close to New Orleans during the yellow fever epidemic makes a certain bizarre sense, so alarmed at the time was the local population about contamination.

Nobody suspected that only a couple of decades later, a much more lethal pestilence was to overtake the city.

"*Ne touche pas,*" Mémère would scold me during our walks through the neighborhood. "*Tu touches tout, et c'est sale* ça." As a boy, I felt compelled to reach out and touch every oak tree, iron fence post, and abandoned tricycle along our path, to form a tactile relationship with the world. But for a woman of her historical era, Mémère was right. Behavior learned during a plague seems to follow people for a lifetime. In September of 1918, when a surge of the Spanish influenza epidemic tore through New Orleans for a terrifying three weeks, my grandmother would have been a recently married twenty-five-year-old, the target age demographic for infection. And she obviously had been told that every surface was contaminated with deadly influenza germs, as many believe today about the coronavirus, insisting as we do on squirting sanitizer on fingers and repeated hand washings. When I lived with Mémère as a high school student during the sixties, the Spanish flu epidemic seemed as ancient to me as the texts I was reading in Latin class about Cesar's Gallic wars, and I couldn't understand why she was such a maniac about disinfecting everything. Once a day she even swabbed the telephone mouthpiece with alcohol.

Although I never saw this austere Creole lady wear a mask, either a bejeweled Mardi Gras one or any other kind, face masks were in wide use during the epidemic of the so-called "sneeze malady," which caused 3,362 deaths in New Orleans between the fall and spring of 1918–19, and 675,000 deaths nation wide. The global mortality toll of this pandemic is estimated at fifty million. Since the contagion arrived in the city onboard a navy ship returning from South America, only military bases and navy stations were quarantined, but schools, movie theaters, and dance halls were closed. Yet the massive war relief rallies and parades, during which people flocked to support the troops and buy Liberty Bonds, caused a wildfire spread of the virus. Mémère never spoke of the epidemic, but did demand that both my grandfather and I wash our hands with soap and hot water before sitting down at *her* table. "I'll wash my hands," was my grandfather's sassy retort, "but I won't use soap." Both this budding teenage beatnik and his whimsical eighty-seven-year-old grandfather thought that Mémère's dictatorial sanitation regime, an obsessive behavior ingrained in her during the flu epidemic, was a real drag. After all, as far as I was concerned, the times they were a'changing.

The times always change, but once traumatized, people seldom do. We can recover from diseases, but a visceral terror, once awakened, will seize us forever. What I learned from these older family members, as well as from both Defoe's and Camus's novels, is that, like war and natural disasters, if plagues don't kill you, they can cause lifelong personality disorders. I wonder if I'll spend the remainder of my days surrounded by skittish people scarred by self-isolation and distrust, socially distanced for life like those lone figures staring out through window panes in Edward Hopper paintings. Many have already become digital versions of Emily Dickinson, and like the reclusive nineteenth-century poet who insisted on whispering to her visitors from around corners, now avoid any face-to-face or voice-to-voice personal contact in favor of the glowing screens of electronic communication.

In my readings of purple and scarlet plague literature, I've discovered that each epidemic leaves the lingering imprint of an aesthetic pathology, a profile of the individual attacked from within, in the same way that war literature leaves a unique image of how societies react when besieged from without. Just as those isolated figures in Hopper's paintings staring vacantly through windows seem emblematic of the coronavirus, the ethereal pallor of Mimi in Puccini's *La bohème* captures the haunting tragedy of the young dying from tuberculosis. The stench of decay that Mann conjures in *Death in Venice* calls to mind the very fetor of cholera, in which the contaminated backwaters of the toothless poor invade the garden parties of the wealthy. Yellow fever is a swamp miasma, buzzing with insidious insects, in the simmering stupor of a tropical summer. And the ancient curses of the Black Death and smallpox represent the crippling disfigurement of the once perfect human form, Adam and Eve covering with fig leaves their bubonic buboes and pustules of pox as they stumble exiled from the Garden of Eden.

In the same way that war tends to unite people, epidemics separate them. If an enemy sniper shoots off my arm or a foreign plane bombs my city, I know whom to accuse and can identify my allies and foes. But when my own body betrays me, invaded from within by some communicable pathogen, and the contagion comes from those closest to me, whom do I blame? The intrusive virus, or my neighbor and friend?

Albert Camus's *The Plague* begins with hundreds of bleeding dead rats. The real rats, as we later find out, are the narrator's fellow citizens, not unlike the shoppers today at my neighborhood grocery, who scurry away from each other with beady rodent eyes staring out above flimsy cotton face masks.

5

First it was iron lungs.

Then the purple blotches of Kaposi's sarcoma.

And now respirators.

This is the third epidemic I've lived through, and my own demographic at the time of each infection has been the targeted one.

I was entering kindergarten in the fall of 1952 during the height of the polio epidemic. That year there were 58,000 new cases of that form of infantile paralysis among kids my age, and 3,000 deaths. My parents had been cautious about letting my sister and me play outside during the summer, and I wasn't sure why. Swimming pools were closed, along with most children's playgrounds in parks. What I remember most vividly are the black-and-white photos from *Life* magazine they showed us of little boys and girls in iron lungs, those metallic coffin-like tubes from which only the child's head emerged. How do they hold an ice cream cone, I wondered, or pick their noses? Before I scampered off to grammar school, I was issued a list of stern do's and don'ts, most of which I can't remember because, dreamy boy that I was, I paid no attention to the do's and did all of the don'ts. I was warned to avoid other children who walked funny, because they might have polio.

"If you get too close to them you might wind up in an iron lung like those pictures in the magazine," my mother said. "And you wouldn't want that, would you?"

From what I remember, my best friend in second grade was a Dutch boy named Derrick who had a lazy foot that dragged behind him. This was the year before we were vaccinated in 1955 with Dr. Jonas Salk's magic pink sugar cubes. Derrick and I walked around the schoolyard with our arms around each other's necks, making up nonsense songs while I ignored his distinct limp. He told me about the windmills and fields of red tulips in Holland, where he'd been sick but recovered. He also said that his family had escaped from the Nazi bad guys, which was why they came to the United States. I can still see his tawny face scrunched up in a broad smile, his complexion more Mediterranean than Nordic. Actually, now that I think of it, he looked Jewish, although then I wouldn't have known what that meant. We had many adventures together, went all over the city on our own, and I felt a real bond with him, closer than to any other kid my age.

The first batch of Dr. Salk's vaccines in 1954 didn't work, and 200,000 children were injected with the defective doses. Thousands of new polio cases developed among those unwitting guinea pigs. To show the skeptical world that the initial vaccine worked, Dr. Alton Ochsner, founder of Ochsner Clinic in New Orleans, had been among the first to have his daughter vaccinated in 1954. She soon died of polio.

Decades later my mother, a hypochondriac obsessed with the medical world, would become the secretary to the poor girl's brother, Dr. John Ochsner, who by then was the director of his father's ever-expanding clinic. At some point after I moved home to New Orleans in 1996, my mother asked me with an amused smile if I remembered my imaginary friend from grammar school. After my thirty years on the road, she and I were getting to know each other again.

"I had an imaginary friend?" I didn't recall that at all.

"You don't remember? You went on and on about him, dreamed up stories about you two gallivanting all over town. You probably made him up because you felt so lonely at first going off to school. His name was Derrick and you said he was Dutch. Holland was always your favorite part of 'Bozo the Clown Goes Around the World,' that record that came with the pretty picture book, remember? We played that part about the windmills and tulips over and over. You said Derrick promised to take you there."

This was news to me: had I made up Derrick? "Did I mention he'd had polio?"

"Oh come on! You made up an imaginary friend with polio?" My mother shot me an alarmed look.

"And the more I think about it, his parents were Jews who had survived Nazi concentration camps."

Born in 1947, I grew up in the shadow of the Holocaust. During the war, my father liberated the concentration camp at Leipzig, and I'd come across a shoebox of horrifying photos of the mounds of skeletal remains that the soldiers immediately had to bury. Thousands of these photographs were distributed to the troops because they suspected nobody would believe what they'd witnessed. My father seldom spoke of it, but his war experience was a dark cloud hovering over the house.

"An imaginary Dutch friend with polio? Whose Jewish family was in a concentration camp? As if he were Anne Frank's brother?" My mother's brow furrowed. "What in the world is wrong with you?"

She never could figure that out.

It appears that I dealt with the deep-seated fear we children felt at the time about getting polio by adopting an imaginary friend who had recovered from the disease. And as a Victory baby, my profound unease about the war and its "Nazi bad guys" had given his family a Holocaust background. I'd made peace with my worst nightmares by letting my overactive imagination turn holy terror into fraternal love. Thank you, Derrick, my first real friend, for getting me through the polio epidemic with your limp, as well as your windmills and tulips.

6

During my second epidemic, I didn't need to make up any diseased imaginary friends. In San Francisco during the eighties half of my real friends were dropping dead with AIDS, a virus that has now killed more than thirty million people worldwide.

After two years as a Fulbright professor at the University in Barcelona, I'd returned to live in the city in the fall of 1981, just as the first cases of a mysterious "gay plague" were being reported. At the moment, none of my own friends had it, although I was starting to see skeletal pariahs with purple lesions of Kaposi's sarcoma on their faces, especially in the gay Castro neighborhood. I was shocked when some Chinese passengers strapped on face masks as they rode through the Castro metro station, even though it had already been established that the disease was spread through intimate contact with either blood or semen.

My first friend to die of the "gay plague" was Hibiscus, founder of the gender-bending theater troupe the Cockettes in the early seventies, an era when I was introduced both to bisexuality and the wild tribal counterculture in San Francisco at the time. Hibiscus died in his native New York before much was known about a disease that so far had killed only 121 people globally. His grief-stricken parents sued the hospital where he died, calling for an investigation into the death of this formerly healthy thirty-four-year-old theater icon. This was before the plague striking gay men, prisoners, junkies, and supposedly Haitians was finally named AIDS on July 27, 1982, and linked to sexual contact or intravenous drug use.

During the previous decade, I'd developed a hang-loose bisexuality that oscillated between women and men. I first moved to Barcelona with a dancer girlfriend, Maureen, with whom I'd broken up after becoming involved with a male writer from Mallorca, then left the country in the middle of a fling with a Spanish woman, who later joined me for a few months in San Francisco. Returning home, I was shocked that the joyous sexual liberation of the seventies had turned into a more predatory and promiscuous fetishism, one that included sadomasochism, bondage, all-night bathhouses, and sex clubs. Handcuffs rattling from his epaulets, my downstairs neighbor Reuben would don his black leather gear every weekend to frequent the Cauldron, a sex club where patrons were locked inside from midnight until dawn to act out fantasies involving swings, ropes, bathtubs, zippered masks, clips, clamps, and whips.

Many of the women previously attracted to bisexual men now considered us Typhoid Marys. Some bisexuals went on what people call "the down low," secretly sleeping with both sexes, while others drifted into gay promiscuity. A weekend pickup in a gay bar, or on the bus for that matter, soon took the place of my serial romantic attachments. At the worst possible moment in the history of the epidemic, when little was known about the disease or how to detect or prevent it, I became something of a disco whore.

During the years before the test, everyone in San Francisco was possessed by the same terror, distrust, and confusion we're presently undergoing with the coronavirus pandemic. The clarifying moment arrived with Dr. Gallo's discovery of the HIV virus and the eventual proliferation of a widely available test for the infection, first developed to screen blood products for hemophiliac patients. This allowed gay and bisexual men in San Francisco to take suitable action to deal with their status. If we tested positive for the virus, we learned what symptoms to watch for and how to care both for our own and our partners' health. If negative, we studied safe sex practices to avoid becoming infected. In intimate relations, we were told to treat everyone as if he were positive, because negative guys could become infected from one week to the next. The street wisdom was that we were sleeping with everyone our partners had ever slept with, even last night.

The test results took two weeks, and receiving them was a life-altering event, a possible death sentence. On three consecutive days before learning my own status, I visited the St. Jude shrine at St. Dominic's Catholic Church on Bush Street, lit candles, and obsessively repeated prayers to the saint of impossible cases.

A smiling doctor told me my test result: negative. I've been devoted to St. Jude ever since.

Rather than becoming a "sex negative" celibate, as many HIV-negative men did, I decided to run away from this frightening scenario. I accepted a teaching position at a university in Beijing, where I moved with my dancer girlfriend, Maureen, in 1983. AIDS was unknown in China at the time, and I'd be able to experience Marxist ideology first hand by living in a Communist country. Like many of my most naïve misadventures, it had seemed like a good idea at the time.

The next year, after returning politically chastened to the still raging epidemic in San Francisco, all I wanted to do was isolate myself and read five hundred good books. So during the next three years I prowled the stacks of the Bancroft Library at the University of California, Berkeley, where I received a Javits Fellowship to become a PhD student in comparative literature. When not holed up in my apartment on Telegraph Hill with books about Pablo Neruda and Walt Whitman, I attended numerous memorial services for friends and former lovers who had died of AIDS.

In California people live in midair, which is where they die, making up rituals as they go along. I was disconcerted by the weepy balloon releases, the upbeat brie-and-white-wine "life celebrations," and the homemade ceremonies to scatter ashes that took the place of the traditional wakes, funerals, burials, and repasts that I remembered from New Orleans. One thing I avoided were the suicide parties, during which friends gathered in the living room of a terminal

AIDS patient while he disappeared into his bedroom to overdose on barbiturates. My grief built up collectively, unexpressed, swept under the carpet of a forever-young culture in which death is a dirty word and dying a faux pas.

Again I ran away. And it was in Barcelona during the pre-Olympic year of 1991 that I almost met my maker. Just before I left San Francisco, I'd sat up all night with my downstairs neighbor Reuben, patron of the black leather club the Cauldron, controlling his morphine drip while he lingered in a coma dying of AIDS. I'd never before ushered anyone into the beyond, so sitting across from the hospital gurney parked in his bedroom, I convinced myself that he could still smell and hear. I lit frankincense and read to him from *The Tibetan Book of the Dead*, which guides dying souls through the bardos of the netherworld toward reincarnation. Just after I stepped out of his bedroom to make coffee, he took his last breath. The moment of dying, I've since been told, is as private as going to the bathroom.

Three days later I was on a plane to Madrid, my chest constricted with grief after Reuben's death. I was returning to Spain, grateful to the Fulbright Commission for another round of teaching fellowships, and finally wound up settling in Barcelona for the next five years. Unlike in San Francisco, where most people freely exchanged HIV statuses, in Spain the epidemic was just beginning to be acknowledged. There was little reliable testing, few self-identified AIDS patients, and the topic was still taboo.

For several months I was seeing a much younger Catalan, a handsome, would-be fashion model named Francesc, who treated his American professor boyfriend with a flattering puppy-eyed devotion. After New Year's I staged a *Reyes* or *fête des Rois* soiree for him at my rooftop flat in the seaside town of Sitges. I'd gotten a French king cake and bottles of Catalan champagne, and after we put on the two golden paper crowns that came with the cake and sat staring into each others eyes in the candlelit room overlooking the Mediterranean, my prince finally told me the truth.

Several months before we met, he'd tested positive for HIV.

"How dare you not let me know!" I leaped across the table to choke him. "I'm going to murder you, *hijo de puta*, before your damn virus has the chance to kill me."

"I thought you'd understand." He was in tears. "I've been careful to practice only safe sex with you."

I thought back: no condoms, but then again no anal penetrations. Little oral-genital contact, but lots of kissing. So far we'd received conflicting messages about whether the virus could be transmitted not just by semen but also by saliva. But once, I remembered, the young man had accidentally ejaculated into my eye. It was messy, and at the moment seemed hilarious, but now it occurred to me that I was doomed.

That *Reyes* evening I didn't kill Francesc, but read him the riot act about informing partners from the beginning about his HIV status and explained that in ethical consideration positives usually sought other positive men for sexual contact, so as not to infect partners by accident, like coming in their eyes.

The next morning I walked with him to catch the train back to Barcelona, noticing how abnormally thin he was, studying every mark on his face for lesions, and wondering if his cough was a first symptom of Pneumocystis.

Much like during the current pandemic, we targeted groups were filled with paranoid delusions about how and why we were being attacked. At the time I felt so helpless and distrustful about the government's response to the AIDS epidemic I subscribed to a prevalent conspiracy theory that HIV had escaped from the US Army Biological Laboratory at Fort Detrick, Maryland. One suspicion was that the virus first had been tested on prisoners, thus quickly spreading among homosexuals, Blacks, and intravenous drug users, groups that represented a significant intersection of jail populations and AIDS victims. Not that there were a lot of incarcerated gay men, but straight cellmate rape victims and so-called "prison bitches" often reemerged in the gay scene as rough trade hustlers. Back in San Francisco, I'd kept a folder of clippings that supposedly proved this nefarious plot. So I wasn't surprised when my friend Toni Morrison, a frequent guest lecturer at the University of Barcelona, agreed with me over dinner one evening as we whispered about the conspiratorial origins of AIDS, as widely believed in both the gay and Black communities.

Only years later did I learn that the Fort Detrick theory was a Cold War disinformation campaign generated by the KGB and the

East German Stasi. Known as Operation Denver, this interference or "active measure" by a foreign power achieved some degree of public credibility by making it as far as a Dan Rather report on the *CBS Evening News*.

Yet at the time, feeling persecuted, I decided to wait out the requisite six months of celibacy before taking another HIV test and to do so at a state-of-the-art hospital in San Francisco. My mother's acute hypochondria kicked in. I was convinced that a purple bruise under my fingernail was a Kaposi's sarcoma lesion. I felt alternately fatigued and angry. I ate compulsively, so as not to waste away. After a visit from my friend, the poet and publisher Lawrence Ferlinghetti, I threw myself into a translation for City Lights Books of the selected poems of the great contemporary poet from Barcelona, Jaime Gil de Biedma, who had died from AIDS only two years earlier. How else in Spain could I make friends with the unmentionable disease that I might be harboring?

I also made friends with Jaime Gil de Biedma's surviving partner, a Catalan actor named Pep Madern, to whom I confessed the agony that Francesc was putting me through.

"Why didn't he tell me from the beginning that he was positive?" I ranted. "Murderer!"

Pep flinched, as if slapped across the face. This obviously was a subject close to his heart. The next spring he also died of AIDS, three years after his poet lover did, and it was anybody's guess which one of the couple infected the other.

From January 6 of that disruptive year until June, when I escaped the galloping greed of the 1992 Olympics in Barcelona and spent the summer back in San Francisco, I underwent a chaste six months of pre-test jitters and self-recriminating meditations. How could I have been such a fool, thinking I could escape from the epidemic that had killed so many of my friends?

Although I'd never been militant about AIDS, I returned to San Francisco at a politically fraught moment, as ACT UP and the Gay Men's Health Crisis continued their activist mobilizations to demand the approval of experimental antiretroviral drugs. The mood at the time is best dramatized in Tony Kushner's *Angels in America,* a play that premiered on Broadway in May of 1991, a year before I arrived in San Francisco for an HIV test. Swords drawn, Kushner's stage was a perfect setting for my own ordeal. Pryor, an angry protagonist crippled with AIDS, asserts, "This disease will be the end of many of us, but not nearly all . . . and we are not going away. We won't die secret deaths anymore." The target of this gay militant wrath was none other than Dr. Anthony Fauci, the present coronavirus czar, then in charge of the indifferent federal response to AIDS. This was after AZT, the treatment approved by the FDA in 1987, had failed, killing more patients than it saved, such as the commie-witch-hunt lawyer Roy Cohn, Donald Trump's mentor and prototype. This dying old demagogue is portrayed in Kushner's play as hoarding a locked stash of AZT in his AIDS hospital room, ranting that "Americans have no use for sick," much like the blustering Trump with his equally toxic hydroxycloroquine. This was before the first introduction of the life-saving cocktail of protease inhibitors was granted an early release in 1995. This miracleonly occurred when the explosive Larry Kramer, head of ACT UP and author of *Faggots*, cornered the cowering Dr. Fauci in his Washington, DC, office and, unlikely as it may have seemed, the two became friends.

At the time, as an expatriate living in Spain, I was fairly oblivious to the politics of the epidemic in the United States. After making my HIV test appointment, I worked with Ferlinghetti on editing the Jaime Gil de Biedma manuscript, and made several pilgrimages to the St. Jude shrine at St. Dominic's. I knew that my life was about to be changed drastically. And it was, at Presbyterian Hospital when I received the test result.

Once again: negative.

Dazed, I wandered from the hospital on Pacific Avenue toward Clement Street, mumbling prayers of thanks. I berated myself for not being more supportive of poor Francesc back in Barcelona, who had given this forty-five-year-old the mortality shock of his life. I vowed to . . . well, I vowed many things that I can't remember and can't answer now as to whether I've kept them.

Strolling down nearby Clement Street in search of some place at which to have a celebratory lunch, I spotted two former lovers of mine huddled over a table inside the Burma Superstar restaurant. There sat Brinda, a woman from India with whom I'd been together for several years before the return to Barcelona, together with Ulysses from Louisiana, a man with whom I'd set out for San Francisco decades ago.

When I burst from the sidewalk into their lunch, they could tell by my beaming smile that my news was good. They'd been worried about me, they confessed, and had met to decide what to do if the results were otherwise. I wrapped them in a cherishing hug. This was how love was supposed to turn out.

The next year my translations of the Spanish poet who died of AIDS came out with City Lights, and the name of Jaime Gil de Biedma, revered in Spain, was introduced to the English-speaking world. While working on the anthology that I titled *Longing*, I'd become intensely involved not only with Jaime's lyric language but with the wry, rebellious persona of this left-wing dandy. We became poet buddies. I often spoke and argued with him in Spanish: why was he so damn indirect, requiring so much clarification on my part? Didn't he understand how difficult it can be to convey the irony of his beloved British poets in the Spanish language? As with Derrick during the polio epidemic, I dealt with my fear of the disease by adopting an imaginary best friend who'd had it. Much like the two lovers in his poem "Anniversary Song," we shifted "from betrayal to boredom, / boredom back to betrayal." And by boredom, I mean wrestling with the tedious subtleties of linguistic parallels, and by betrayal, the inspired yet inevitable rewriting that one poet often succumbs to when translating another.

When I first met Pep, Jaime's surviving partner, he'd greeted me with an amused grin. "Funny," he said, "that you're Jaime's translator, because you're exactly his type. He couldn't have kept his eyes off you."

7

Last weekend a neighbor of mine had to drive all the way from New Orleans to Baton Rouge to be tested for coronavirus. He tested negative and was prescribed antibiotics for his routine pulmonary ailments. As with the AIDS epidemic, until a reliable test for the coronavirus is widely available, we'll continue to cower from the disease in mortal fear and unnerving confusion. Once the general population is tested, positives as well as those with a weakened immune system should continue to self-isolate while negatives return to their public lives.

Sweden has been criticized for its socially unrestrictive "herd immunity" approach to this pandemic, although 75 percent of Swedes agree with this policy. Sweden has increased its testing capacity to 100,000 people weekly, and there employees are provided with take-home test kits twice a month, the most sensible solution I've heard so far. In what now seems like a parallel universe, those with healthy immune systems are encouraged to mingle in cafes, bars, and restaurants to self-immunize. My San Francisco friend Birgitta, a registered nurse originally from Stockholm, tells me that "at first I thought the Swedes were out of their minds. The country does have one of the lowest per capita death rates from the virus in Europe, but still more than other Scandinavian countries in lockdown. Most of the deaths have been in nursing homes. But the jury is still out. Of course, we Swedes not only practice social distancing, we've perfected it. It's in our blood."

I understand why the vulnerable population should self-isolate, as well as those already infected. As it has in China, this epidemic will mutate and reoccur, we don't know when or where, and when it does, won't these pure, untouched individuals be like lambs led to the slaughter?

A lot of people must be self-immunized and don't know it. Thankfully there's a reliable five minute test for this seroconversion coming out, but much too slowly, like everything else. Immune systems are strengthened by rising to health challenges, not by hiding away like the boy with zero immunity forced to live inside a plastic bubble. The basis of immunology is the old adage that whatever doesn't kill you will make you stronger, so some risk is involved. Survival itself is a risky business. I've tested positive, for instance, for exposure to tuberculosis (after living in China), malaria (after my travels in India), as well as hepatitis B (after my disco whore days in San Francisco), but have never developed any of those diseases. I probably have antibodies for typhoid and cholera also. My test results for exposure light up the tropical disease charts. Try self-isolating in a packed bus in China, India, or South America. Isn't the gradual self-immunization of the general population a good thing to slow down epidemics?

The current coronavirus mitigation model is borrowed from a totalitarian country, one I know only too well, where citizens do exactly as they're told and are inured to government lies, subterfuge, and wildly erratic political agendas. In general, the Chinese have a difficult time understanding Western individuality and identify strongly with the collective values of family, community, and traditional culture, for the benefit of which they'll sacrifice anything. My graduate students in Beijing couldn't quite grasp British Romantic poetry. So what if Shelley falls "upon the thorns of life" and bleeds, they argued, since he'll live on in his children. Trying to import public health policy from a country of "we" and "our" to fit a culture of "I" and "mine" is a difficult translation. In Wuhan, nobody objected when those infected with the virus were welded inside their apartments with outside door bolts. The Chinese are used to having their individual rights trampled on.

Willingly or not, they're accustomed to being civic doormats.

Of course, this policy of social distancing and quarantine didn't originate in China but during the wildly misguided bubonic plague epidemics, as portrayed in the novels of Defoe and Camus. Now we know why it didn't work. The plague wasn't spread by personal contagion but by flea bites from black rats while frightened people self-isolated in their rat-infested houses. Are we really any smarter during the current plague? Or as a friend recently told me, "Look, I'm really sorry about the twenty thousand Americans who so far have died of this disease. But even if we can save the kitten trapped inside, is it worth letting the whole house burn down?"

Ironically, the woman who made this seemingly callous comment is the daughter of one of my oldest friends, JoAnna, the only person I know who has died of the coronavirus. I first met JoAnna when I was seventeen, a defiant highschool student hanging out with older bohemian artists in the French Quarter. Now eighty-three years old, JoAnna entered Touro Hospital at the beginning of February to receive a transfusion for a blood clot. There she sickened considerably, developing a constant cough, a high fever, and was unable to breath. The doctors said she wasn't getting enough oxygen and had developed pneumonia, even as she begged her family gathered around the hospital bed to get her the hell out of there. She died while they were trying to intubate her to connect a respirator. This was on February 14, ten days before Mardi Gras, and the doctors had yet to diagnose coronavirus patients. They didn't know what new condition she'd developed in the hospital, but there was no doubt she got it there. Her death occurred during the same week as other unreported mortalities from the virus in Santa Clara, California.

Her funeral was held two weeks later, on February 29. Leave it to that feisty romantic to pass away during Carnival, on Valentine's Day, no less, then to have a funeral on Saddie Hawkins Day, only to miss the present lockdown, which would have left her livid with indignation. Little did we know at the time, but as we friends kissed and hugged her large family during the funeral repast, it was like a children's measles or "pox party," when kids are brought into proximity of an infected measles carrier to acquire self-immunity. After JoAnna's death, several of her family members did develop mild flu-like symptoms, but this was before the pandemic was acknowledged, and they though little of it.

JoAnna was always the first person I knew to try anything different, from selling her paintings on Jackson Square during the sixties to more recently, as a beaming great-grandmother hobbling along on a walker, hanging out with gutterpunks at a rowdy café on Decatur Street.

And now I like to imagine that she lives on in me in the form of coronavirus antibodies.

8

As for the leadership of the sociopath in the White House who stumbles through incoherent press briefings trying to prop up his failing administration, what more can be said? One letter to the *Washington Post* parodies Trump's comments if he were the captain of the Titanic:

> There isn't any iceberg. There was an iceberg but it's in a
> totally different ocean. The iceberg is in this ocean but it

will melt very soon. There is an iceberg but we didn't hit the iceberg. We hit the iceberg, but the damage will be repaired very shortly. The iceberg is a Chinese iceberg. We are taking on water but every passenger who wants a lifeboat can get a lifeboat, and they are beautiful lifeboats. Look, passengers need to ask nicely for the lifeboats if they want them. We don't have any lifeboats, we're not lifeboat distributors. Passengers should have planned for icebergs and brought their own lifeboats. I really don't think we need that many lifeboats and they're supposed to be our lifeboats, not the passenger's lifeboats. The lifeboats were left on shore by the last captain of this ship. Nobody could have foreseen this iceberg.

Today I saw a McDonald's home-delivery commercial on TV: "Your country needs you to stay on your sofa." This tagline is followed by a series of couch potatoes giving crisp military salutes, doing their patriotic duty by scarfing Big Macs as the ship goes down.

The message: *we need to come together by staying apart.* I tried that once with phone sex, and it didn't work.

9

Gun violence is the most persistently menacing epidemic in the US, yet public policy is hands-off: don't abridge anyone's personal rights by taking away their stockpile of AK-47s. In 2019 more than 30,000 Americans were killed by firearms, either in homicides or suicides. And according to the epidemiologist Philip Alcabes, worldwide yearly deaths from vehicle crashes are estimated at 1.35 million, and now curable tuberculosis kills more than a million people annually. Deaths from diarrhea top 1.5 million. "These tolls will continue," he writes in *The American Scholar*. "They will never be called epidemics. They will be allowed to be meaningless."

The government response to the coronavirus, according to Alcabes, "has been to isolate ourselves, even to force people into isolation. Yet isolation itself is grueling, sometimes mortally so. The isolation means that we can't even witness the deaths of our family members."

Or as I've just discovered, we can't visit the graves of long-deceased ancestors. Yesterday, on Holy Saturday, I brought Easter lilies to our family tomb in the cemetery next door. I said a few prayers for their eternal rest, with a whispered aside to the four generations buried there that I just might be joining them soon. I thought of my mother, who had been living in an old folks' home (call it "assisted living" or a "care community," whatever makes you feel better), when she passed away in 2003. Were she there now, nobody would be allowed to visit her, and she'd be suffering alone.

As I approached the spiked iron cemetery gate, I was startled to see it closed. I was locked inside the graveyard. Running between the tombs in a panic, I finally spotted a custodian's white pickup and asked him to let me out.

"I really don't want to be locked in a cemetery during a global plague. The gates are supposed to be open until 4:30," I said, pointing at the visitors sign facing the street.

"The archdiocese done closed this cemetery count of the virus," the custodian said. "Only reason I had the gate open was there was a burial here this afternoon. You're lucky you found me. Gate be open tomorrow morning but only for Easter Sunday."

"I had no idea," I sputtered, "that social distancing applied to the dead and buried. My mother died of heart failure seventeen years ago, which is what you almost gave me."

I wasn't angry at either the custodian or the archdiocese, but at the passive, unthinking mindset that would make the absurdity of closing a nineteenth-century cemetery a part of public health policy. It's not as if people go to the cemetery to hang out with the living, although here in New Orleans families do gather there on All Saints' Day. Yet there's already enough social distance between the living and the dead that we don't need any more painful reminders.

Easter Sunday, April 12, 2020: There have been 22,000 coronavirus deaths nationwide. In Italy, drones patrol for smoke that might signal family barbecue gatherings on rooftop terraces. In Savannah drones also scan the neighborhoods for holiday get-togethers. The police pull a man not wearing a face mask from public transit in Philadelphia. Camus's protagonist, Dr. Rieux, notes that the ancient Chinese played tambourines to dispel the germs of a plague and wonders whether "in practice, tambourines provided more efficacious prophylactic measures than our own."

10

People suffering from depression often isolate themselves from friends and family, and the retreat from the world around them deepens their depression into a downward spiral of inner darkness and despair. Unruly prisoners are put in solitary confinement for long periods of time as a form of punishment, which many criminologists consider a cruel and unusual one. The goal is to break their spirits and force them into utter passivity. And it works.

It's the day after Easter, and this year the stone has not been rolled away from the mouth of the tomb.

No resurrection is in sight from the past forty days of penitent Lent. The Lenten period of forty days is the root of the word quarantine, from the Latin number *quadraginta,* adopted into English from the French word for forty, *quarante,* and the Italian *quarantino.*

Along with millions of others, I'm still inside the tomb staring at the stone blocking the entrance. "Anxiety itself is getting tired," as Lorrie Moore writes in the *New Yorker,* "and when anxiety gets tired it turns into despair." Or as Camus observes in *The Plague,* "The habit of despair is worse than despair itself." He describes a seemingly endless quarantine during which the population is "listless, indifferent, and looking so bored . . . that the whole town seemed like a railway waiting-room."

I'm one of the 30 percent of Americans who live alone, a number that climbs to almost 50 percent among those of us in our seventies. I'm not of a depressive nature, more on the manic side, if you want to know the truth. My writing requires long periods of structured solitude, but when not working I'm a social person. Now I find myself sleeping more than usual, and it's harder to get out of bed. I prefer my vivid, lively dreams to waking reality, which stretches far into an uncertain future with an unbearable drone. "Yes, plague, like abstraction," notes Camus, "was monotonous." Last night I dreamed that I was keeping a hamster in a cage in which I was delighted to discover another hamster alongside him. Where did this new company come from, I wondered, and who put it there?

Then I woke up, alone in my cage. No unseen hand had provided any companion.

I wonder if public health administrators have foreseen the long-term effects of mandatory self-isolation on those of us living alone. At times this house arrest feels like a penitentiary-style punishment, and at others like an inexorable decline into depression. I resist the distraction of videoconferencing—the online music festivals, exercise classes, poetry readings, and Zoom sessions—which only make me feel more acutely my distance from the outside world, adding a pixilated insult to the injury of not really being together. Voyeurism is the most depressing form of excitement. Except when writing, every moment not spent staring at a computer screen is sheer paradise. I'd rather gaze at the breeze stirring the live oak branches outside my window than at Lady Gaga trying to entertain me on the lit electronic rectangle of my laptop.

One friend, a travel agent, has already been told that from now on her job will consist of working from home. My greatest fear, in fact, isn't of dying, but that this pandemic will become the gateway drug toward a new normal ever more reliant on videoconferencing and other forms of virtual reality. I dread the moment when we abandon our mammalian herd instincts and move into the hive consciousness of insect social organization, our digital antennae ever tuned like ants and bees into the Wi-Fi waves of the group mind. Because of our biology, humans aren't meant to log on and swarm, but rather to nuzzle and frolic.

The clinical depression and high suicide rates among those isolated teenagers addicted to their iPhones have been documented with increasing alarm. Now their grim existence is being forced upon the rest of us, supposedly to save our lives.

In 1909 E.M. Forster published a science fiction novella called *The Machine Stops*, a chillingly prescient look at a society in which people, afflicted with a "horror of direct experience," live alone in subterranean pods staring at the illuminated screens in their laps, projections of a centralized Machine programmed to meet all their needs. Communication with others takes place through transmitted images, what we now call videoconferencing, and they "never touched one another. The custom has become obsolete, owing to the

Machine." Although people may occasionally whoosh through tubes in airborne cylinders from one pod to a more distant one, they never set foot on the supposedly unlivable surface of the earth, currently known as the brick-and-mortar world. That is a forbidden realm, one in which those few who have permanently escaped the screen-in-pod existence are called the "homeless." In these transport cylinders, the socially distanced passengers "sat each in his cabin, avoiding one another with an almost physical repulsion and longing to be once more under the surface of the earth."

The people isolated in their underground pods spend their days absorbed by the lectures and forums that appear on their screens. One such content provider warns his public to "beware of first hand ideas." All aspects of this voyeuristic existence are translated by the Machine into its own one-dimensional terms for an audience that has gotten "beyond the facts, beyond impressions, a generation absolutely colorless, a generation seraphically free from any hint of personality," one that sees "the French Revolution not as it happened, nor as they would like it to have happened, but as it would have happened had it taken place in the days of the Machine."

Then this all-encompassing form of artificial intelligence, or AI as we now know it, breaks down. The omnipotent Machine abruptly crashes, leaving nobody or nothing to contact with a query or complaint. The robot voices are silenced; all lit screens go blank. No longer provided with climate control or food deliveries slipped into their door slots, people scrambling to escape their failing pods are forced to crawl toward the Earth's surface over the corpses of those who have already died.

In a plague.

The final sight of the protagonist is of tree limbs framed in the cerulean blue sky arching above her.

If Forster could imagine this dystopian new normal in 1909, why can't we see it now?

And the cruel irony is that we're being forced into the mental and physical illness of this screen-in-pod existence supposedly for our health.

11

During this third week in April, angry protests against the lock-down have broken out across the country, both in Democratic and Republican states. A deafening polarization is growing between those who demand that the restrictions end soon and those who fear they won't continue long enough. The worse aspect of the protests, according to some commentators, is that the participants aren't standing six feet apart and wearing face masks. This observation misses their point. They are fed up with these rules and are insisting that life return to normal, in spite of the 44,000 people who so far have died of the virus in the United States.

Although the protestors ostensibly seem aligned with the business-oriented Trump administration rather than the public health policies of Democrats, I suspect they are drawn from across the political spectrum. These people are in no way, as they've been called, "pro-virus," an absurd accusation. They themselves might be infected or have lost loved ones to the disease. The hungry have no political agenda except to eat, and heartbreaking automotive bread lines of the unemployed are causing traffic jams in front of free food pantries. Some people are standing up for what they call "liberty" while others are waiting for a few boxes of food.

Before the lockdown rules enforced during this pandemic, my three previous experiences in highly restrictive societies were periods spent living in both right-wing and left-wing dictatorships. In the early seventies I visited Franco's Spain for two months, mostly hiding out in the beach house of Jimmy Page of the Led Zeppelin and with other international hippies on the swinging island of Ibiza. Yet even there the *guardias civiles* would shoot to kill nude beachgoers, without warning, no questions asked. In Barcelona there was a strictly enforced curfew to rid the country of dissident Communist cells. Those returning home after lockdown would first have to locate a neighborhood *sendero,* a guide who would study their documents and escort them to their front doors, which these guides would unlock with government-issued skeleton keys.

In the mid-1970s I lived for several months under a military state of siege in Colombia, during which jumpy teenage soldiers were stationed with menacing rifles on every corner. At any point a bus or train could be stopped, emptied, and searched. When traveling between towns, we had to pass through checkpoints where soldiers demanded documents and pawed through our belongings. This ostensibly was to crack down on guerrilla movements at the beginning of a burgeoning civil war in Latin America that lasted for decades, now referred to as the Dirty War.

In China during the early eighties our phones were bugged, letters opened, and visitors to our foreigners' compound forced to register with Red Guards at the front gate. All meetings with Chinese friends were secretly organized and clandestine. The politically correct term for the Halloween party I staged at our university was "cultural pollution." Of course, I wasn't allowed to teach George Orwell's *Nineteen Eighty-Four* in 1984, and the book was stricken from my graduate student syllabus. According to the Communist Party, this level of control was to protect the well-being of the People from Capitalist-Roader nationals as well as the Big Noses, as we foreigners were called.

My experiences in these tightly regimented countries cut across the political gamut, from Right to Left. Frankly, I saw no difference. All three dictatorships manipulated the masses to justify their oppressive regulations with hysterical fear—of dissidents, guerrillas, or capitalist foreigners.

One major difference between those restrictive regimes and the present one is that then, of course, I could leave each of these countries, which I did. Now I can't. There's nowhere else to go, except perhaps Sweden. So when I observe the rabid faces of the lockdown protestors, I understand them, without assigning either blame or ideology. In each of the three dictatorships in which I lived, there were pockets of underground resistance, and eventually in Spain and Colombia they won. Unfortunately in China, not yet. But I instinctively distrust any authority that obliges me to act against my will for my own good or to obey some patriotic dictate for what I'm told benefits the collective well-being.

In *The Plague*, Camus uses a town's oppressive quarantine edicts to contain the bubonic plague as an extended metaphor for open-ended Fascist rule, specifically of Nazi-occupied France during World

War II. If the shoe fits, I'm afraid we'll have to wear it. Down to the last detail, the political and interpersonal environment he describes is strikingly similar to our present one, including the contradictory medical information the government issues and the dedicated but exhausted hospital staff. I'm much less afraid of dying from the coronavirus than of people gradually accepting this degree of political and social control "for your own good."

This is the dilemma that public health now faces as its lockdown mandates provoke an epidemic of suicide among socially alienated young people, alone with their phones, and spike a mass of premature deaths among the isolated elderly, not allowed to visit with their grandkids, much less each other.

Should pandemic policies attempt to save our lives even if they kill us?

In the panic after 9/11, we accepted the TSA controls at airports mandated by the so-called Patriot Act, even as they were expanded to include such absurdities as banning bottles of water or shampoo or the indignities of intimate pat downs. Now such routine checkpoint searches are in place on entering most public buildings, even during the Louisiana State Book Festival in Baton Rouge. I wonder if there's much international terrorism targeting provincial book festivals. We've become so accustomed to accommodating these restrictions that we've lost sight of their original objectives.

In a power grab justified by controlling the coronavirus, President Viktor Orbán of Hungary has dissolved the parliament, which has granted him the unlimited authority to rule by decree, with no sunset clause. Hungarian officials claim that similar COVID-19 coups d'état have taken place in Croatia, Poland, and Malta. In Latin America, the Salvadoran military are using lockdown laws as a pretext for patrolling the streets to round up and imprison young men whom they suspect might be associated with gangs, as if crowded jail cells would better protect them from contagion than circulating in the open air outside of their homes, probably looking for food to feed their families. As Camus points out in *The Plague*, the problem during a pandemic isn't in the public health protocols themselves but rather in the unbridled power granted to those who enforce them.

In 1935 Sinclair Lewis published *It Can't Happen Here*, a novel about a Fascist takeover of the United States, in which he vividly imagines a scenario that disproves the clichéd title. In an introduction to the Signet edition, Michael Meyer sets the scene of Sinclair's thirties background in terms immediately recognizable today: "Many who were solid, respectable breadwinners found themselves on bread lines, soup lines, and relief rolls. 'Normalcy,' a twenties password synonymous with security, gave way to the 'jitters' as profitless corporations laid off millions of workers."

The "jitters" is a perfect word to describe the new normal. It is, as Meyer puts it, "fascism masquerading in a patriotic costume."

Today I noticed that the leafy triangular park in front of our neighborhood grocery had been closed off with forbidding chain-link fencing. The grocer informed me that neighbors had complained about people gathering there in groups of more than ten, above the requisite limit said to be a threat to our health. Some of my more entitled neighbors had been trying for years to rid that park of its grizzled winos, harmless old locals seated in a circle of lawn chairs who merrily greeted me as I waited for the bus. Now these snooty neighbors had a perfect excuse, as do the states of Texas and Arkansas to suspend all abortions: our security from the enemy virus.

In every instance, I'd choose freedom over safety from any designated enemy, whether it be communists, guerrillas, spies, and winos.

Or, in this case, a disease, one which Trump calls "the Invisible Enemy." Michel de Montaigne wrote: "He who has learned how to die has unlearned how to be a slave."

Following his advice, I acknowledge that one day I will die, but in the meantime won't accept not being free.

12

We've all got the crazies, not just the street people in the French Quarter.

Friends tell me that the Quarter, a neighborhood where I lived for twenty years, is now not only a ghost town but a zombie apocalypse scenario. The few people left on the sidewalks are deranged street people who scream at passersby. I always assumed the street people had been drawn to the neighborhood to panhandle tourists, but now there are none. So evidently they have nowhere else to go. Those saner folk in the homeless encampments have been relocated to a downtown Hilton, ironically the same hotel where the Amazon vampire movie producers planned to house us tenants from the Luling Mansion during the now-canceled film shoot. Obviously it's the flexible go-to lodging for displaced locals. So the street people drifting around the Quarter are the ones too crazy even to be relocated.

In this topsy-turvy experiment in social restructuring, sane people are now locked up inside while lunatics have taken over the streets.

The lockdown has closed almost all Quarter businesses, except for a handful of small grocery stores, and most shops are boarded up to prevent looting. That's the inevitable next phase that follows abandonment in American cities, as we witnessed after Hurricane Katrina in New Orleans. Once a vibrant bohemian neighborhood of artists, writers, musicians, gays, and preservationists, what the Quarter has become over the past quarter century is now starkly evident: a flim-flam historic backdrop for mass tourism hollowed out of most of its permanent residents. The majority of the occupied apartments are second homes for wealthy out-of-towners who dash in for weekends and festivals, people now holed up in their first homes. A small core of permanent residents remains, whittled down to approximately 850 from the 15,000–20,000 locals who used to call it home. With the recent illegalization of short-term rentals, which made real estate prices prohibitive for locals, the Quarter was just starting to bounce back as a neighborhood again before the pandemic.

I was living there after Katrina, when New Orleans struck me as an open-air mental hospital. Once again madness has taken over, not only the zombie apocalypse loonies wandering Quarter streets but most of us shut up inside our houses. And since we can't gather together to rant and rave, we do so by telephone, email, or social media. Everyone is edgy and tightly wound, divided into two opposing teams: the medical Grim Reapers terrified of falling ill or the economic Doomsdayers angry at the restrictions tanking the economy.

And as after Katrina, there's only one topic of conversation.

One Doomsday friend, whose financial consulting business is faltering, calls me to shout statistics that supposedly prove it's not worth wrecking the country for so few deaths. I speak with another, a science fiction writer convinced that the 5G Wi-Fi towers recently installed for internet access destroy the immune system, causing people to easily fall ill with the infection. A medical Grim Reaper cousin tells me I need to buy a freezer and generator, convinced that food distribution will unravel during the famine after the next outbreak of the disease. You see, he's in contact with scientists in *New York!* he emphasizes—as opposed to, say, those amateur white coats in Chicago or San Francisco—who are assured this pandemic will wipe out a large percentage of the human race. When I counter that I'm not particularly worried about contracting the disease, he reminds me of my age and heart condition. He warns that the virus goes straight to the heart so that—I'm not sure what the point is except that I should panic along with him.

"I understand," I say, trying to console him. "I'll latch my shutters, put on a hazmat suit, and lock myself inside the cedar chest."

I hear that some New Yorkers have stopped going out in the city not to avoid infection but because everyone in the street has become so testy and nasty. The addictive media reports remain unrelenting in their pandemic numbers, as if keeping score. While medical scientists insist we're in the second inning of a nine-inning baseball game, economists predict a deep depression looms if businesses don't open soon. As after the devastation following Katrina, I stand back and try to give everyone I speak with a wide berth of sympathy and compassion. During this divisive election year, Americans are so fiercely polarized about how to deal with the lockdown that the bridge of common humanity between us has collapsed. They can't talk to each other apart from warning about one of two dire outcomes: either you'll starve or you'll die.

The pandemic makes the same threat that every mugger sneers: *your money or your life.*

Yet Doomsday economists also fall ill and die, and Grim Reaper medical scientists have to be paid and eat. We're in this together.

When the president of the United States suggests that we should shoot up Lysol, I throw my hands in the air.

Maintaining perspective has always meant keeping my sense of humor, and even in the normally jolly Big Easy I hear very few virus jokes. President Trump, a gold mine for comics, satirists, and cartoonists, has kept us rolling in the aisles with guffaws for the past three years. But now the laughter has stopped. Spanish friends in Madrid, an epicenter of the pandemic with whom I occasionally speak, have maintained their edge of black humor. In strict lockdown, people there are only allowed on the streets an hour a day to walk their pets. Last week the police detained a pedestrian strolling down the Gran Vía clutching a fishbowl containing his only pet. He was walking his goldfish. And here's a Spanish joke about the virus, loosely translated:

"Guess what? I finally took the test," a man says.

"Oh," his listener replies. "The results?"

"Good. Looks like I'm going to have a girl."

"Happy Jazz Fest!" bellows one of the gristly winos ejected from the park in front of our grocery store. Dagger-eyed people wearing face masks freeze in their tracks to stare at him. This year Jazz Fest is happy enough for me because it isn't happening.

Tonight my Grim Reaper cousin stops by to bring me a supply of my favorite foods from Costco: octopus, prosciutto, other antipasto, and goat cheese. He knows I won't be wearing a mask, but on arriving lowers his and we stand six feet apart chatting at my front gate. I notice what a difference the nuances of a human presence make in communication, the gestures, facial movements, and eye-to-eye contact that modulate words. He and I joke, laugh, even reminisce. We acknowledge each other's vulnerability and humanity with ritual body language, unlike the words yanked out of context in distracting phone confrontations or email snits.

As if to celebrate this moment of rare communion, for some reason a group of kids sets off firecrackers in the middle of the street. And I think of the Chinese use of fireworks to scare off the demons of war, discord, and disease. My cousin's drop-by visit has been one of my few furry moments in this gnawing Year of the Metal Rat.

13

Social distancing began long before the current pandemic, about a decade ago.

In the past week I've only had face-to-face contact with two friends, except for the masked neighborhood grocery clerks. At some point in our conversations both friends pulled out their cells phones to photograph me, a nervous social tic that has become as involuntary as the handshake or a peck on the check. But it breaks the interactive rhythm with the same chilling effect as approaching a police barricade. Suddenly I'm posing, trying to look good.

The first was on my balcony, to which I actually invited someone to have dinner with me. Okay, send out a public health drone or call the police, but after driving me to a distant supermarket, what else could I do? And to my delight, she accepted. Recently a similar invitation prompted the British epidemiologist Neil Ferguson, who spearheaded the strict social distancing policies that locked down England, to resign. His criminal tête-a-tête at home was with a married lover, a tad more titillating than mine.

Right in the middle of the cheese appetizers, my friend took out her phone and took pictures of my plants, my bedroom through the balcony window, and then of me in various reluctant poses. Then as we sat and talked, she brandished the phone in front of her, as if taking a selfie chest x-ray. Finally I begged her to stop videoing me and to place her apparatus on a bamboo tray that I whisked inside.

Over the past decade, I've given up on asking people not to take out their things and play with them in front of me. I realize I'm dealing with a serious neurological condition that others can't control, an addiction stronger than smoking although perhaps less severe than heroin. My only attempt to impose some decorum is the ironclad rule: smoking permitted, but no cell phones or syringes at my dinner table. Within my own home, I allow people five minutes to fiddle with their tech toys before they're banished from my sight. Unfortunately, I've lost several good friends this way, people who couldn't keep their fingers off their junk when sitting face-to-face with me at the table.

The second incident happened just yesterday, while I was trudging down Esplanade Avenue lugging two sacks of groceries. A French Quarter friend and his lady swerved up in a car beside me with effusive greetings. I put down my weighty sacks and we stopped to talk. Then, just as I was cherishing this moment of spontaneous contact, they both pulled out cell phones and started photographing me.

"Oh, it's perfect," the friend said. "This is a portrait for the dust jacket of your next book."

"You at the iron gate in front of the bougainvillea and that wide veranda," enthused his girlfriend, "nobody will believe this in New York."

Both meetings had turned into a scroll-through in which I was merely the visual content. Needless to say, I'll never lay eyes on these friends' photos, but their defensive reaction to another's presence was to brandish an electronic device to distance us: to put on a digital face mask, to control the experience by attempting to capture it.

Don't get me wrong: years ago as a freelance journalist, I lived with and hung out with professional photographers and admire their art form. Cameras in hand, I knew when they were setting up a shot: the lighting, the angle, and the focus. This I understand because it's a discipline. It's art, and that's what I practice and try to perfect.

But this twitchy reaction to another's presence—the need to distance an interaction with an electronic device in order to scroll through it later, to translate the intimate into the virtual—is a contemporary personality disorder.

Social distancing doesn't need a face mask or a six-foot margin between people to change the way we interact. It doesn't need a pandemic and has been with us for a while now.

14

Today I received in the mail my $1,200 "economic impact payment" from President Donald J. Trump, his name printed on the check in the lower-left "for" line. This is a variation on what the Roman politician Cicero called "bread and circuses," which he insisted would satisfy the citizens as their empire crumbled. "The evil wasn't in the bread and circuses," he wrote, "but in the willingness of the people to sell their rights as freemen for full bellies and the excitement of the games."

That master showman Donald Trump is himself the circus, as we witnessed during that misguided TV miniseries of both the Mueller and impeachment hearings.

And now he's sent me my bread.

To celebrate, I set off on my daily trek down Esplanade Avenue to the neighborhood grocery to buy a bottle of Spanish wine. I walk past Santa Fe, a restaurant much enjoyed for its spacious terrace seating and margaritas, if not for its uninspired Tex-Mex food. The restaurant is still open for takeout and home delivery, yet now yellow police caution-tape cordons off the terrace seating. But a group of twelve, maybe fifteen people, is idling on the sidewalk holding cocktails in go-cups or seated with their takeout orders on the four benches under the crepe myrtles on the other side of the sidewalk, sharing food from Styrofoam containers. A tipsy older gentleman backs into me and almost spills his drink as I stride by. I'm pleased to see people enjoying themselves for a change and decide it must be a party to celebrate my stimulus check.

Fifteen minutes later, as I walk past, *five*—I count five—police cars with flashing blue lights have arrived in front of Santa Fe to enforce social distancing regulations and break up this illegal wingding. The restaurant owners, a lovely Turkish woman and her Portuguese husband, are angrily taping scrawled signs on the benches that warn "Do not sit, eat, or drink on these benches!" Arms folded, belligerent-looking officers stand in military formation surrounding the crime scene as takeout diners scurry away. I don't want to linger in this party-pooping dragnet to see if the cops are issuing citations to either the owners or customers. Down the block an officer munching on a taco is flirting with three attractive young women straddling bicycles bunched in a tight circle. From what I can make out, he's explaining something about "groups of ten people or more."

As a non-driver I've been unaware that for two months police checkpoints have been set up throughout the city to stop motorists, examine their licenses, and ask where they are driving and why. Is the trip essential or for leisure? These police checkpoints have been discontinued, I've since learned, but the disturbing concept brings back the military state of siege I endured in Colombia, the curfews in Fascist Spain, and the neighborhood Communist Party snitches in China. I wouldn't be surprised if the entitled neighbors responsible for fencing off the triangular park to dispel winos also called the cops on the spontaneous gathering in front of Santa Fe. Years ago I unsubscribed from those fussbudgets' daily barrage of persnickety neighborhood-watch emails, but I know their type.

Lately I'd been hearing sirens at all hours of the day and night, hoping the Faubourg St. John isn't becoming a new crime hub or pandemic hotspot. It hasn't. I just learned the police have closed off the street alongside Bayou St. John to vehicular traffic because groups of nervy super-spreaders have been driving to the bayou to sit in lawn chairs to talk and—this being New Orleans—probably drink. So sirens blaring, the police have been conducting raids to enforce social distancing among pudgy, middle-class folks dressed in cargo shorts fed up with the lockdown, just as they buzz-killed my stimulus check sidewalk party today.

Whoever would have thought that sedate Bayou St. John would become the new Bourbon Street? This would even puzzle Cicero: people selling their rights as freemen, but for what? Maybe they'd just gotten their bread too and wanted a circus, or more likely just a chat and a hug.

15

Let's try to think like the enemy.

If I were a malevolent virus, I could devise no better means to spread myself into a global pandemic than through mass tourism. What better place to plant my spiky spores than in the recycled air of planes, airports, and cruise ships, those cattle cars in which strangers are herded together for long periods of time? Then I could burst like a handful of viral confetti on the unsuspecting local populations who live near iconic monuments in picture-postcard neighborhoods and at packed festivals. After two or three days, the span of a package travel deal, destination wedding, or cruise ship stopover, my complacent carriers would be gone, crammed back into the same cylinders of contagion that brought them there for their fun-filled getaway.

Meanwhile the locals would sicken and die.

In a front-page *New York Times* article on May 4, the lead questions "Why Does the Virus Wallop Some Places and Spare Others?" The piece explains that the coronavirus "impact has seemed capricious. Global metropolises like New York, Paris, and London have been devastated, while teeming cities like Bangkok, Baghdad, New Delhi and Lagos have, so far, largely been spared." Am I the only reader to discern that the hard-hit cities mentioned are magnets of mass tourism—Times Square and Broadway shows, the Eiffel Tower and Montmartre, Big Ben and Buckingham Palace—while the other jam-packed cities listed are the hardship posts of the hospitality industry?

I've spent time in Bangkok, and except for a booming sex trade and the post-coital Reclining Buddha sculpture at Wat Pho, found that the noisy, chaotic city offers little as a prime travel destination. You can get better Thai food in San Francisco. New Delhi is a dense administrative beehive in India, but except to visit the nearby Taj Mahal, tourists don't flock there. A weekend getaway to Baghdad or Lagos anyone? I doubt it. Individual international travelers may be abundant in those cities, but they have personal business or family connections. They're not planeloads of goggle-eyed foreigners who go everywhere in groups.

The article goes on to mention that unlike nearby Malaysia, "in Indonesia, thousands are believed to have died of the coronavirus." Who hasn't been to Bali, but to Malaysia? Nobody I know. Unlike neighboring Argentina or Bolivia, Brazil is another virus hotspot, but should that surprise any online vacation hunter heading to the beach at Ipenema or to Carnival? Or consider equally devastated Peru, where last year the government considered temporarily closing the ruins of Machu Picchu because of the damage done by an onslaught of tourism. And speaking of onslaughts, besieged Venice is invaded every year by thirty million tourists, most of whom are day-trippers, and the famed city is only a two-hour drive from Lombardy, the first European region to be devastated by the coronavirus.

This massification of leisure travel is a twenty-first-century phenomenon, and nothing better illustrates this phenomenon than any hub airport or glossy brochure destination. Flight and high-rise hotel deals abound, online air prices are rock-bottom, and on cruise ships tourists are stacked in cages like chickens at poultry-processing plants. Rubber-necking double-decker red buses circulate hourly, walking tours clog sidewalks, and Airbnbs have displaced permanent residents from historic neighborhoods. I'm really glad that I traveled as much as I did when younger, at a time when the world still abounded with unexplored places and cozy family-run hotels, and transportation was easy, relaxed, and adventurous.

In his stinging critique of the Gilded Age, Thorstein Veblen was the first to focus on this subject in *The Theory of the Leisure Class*, published in 1899. He pointed out the snob appeal upon which current mass tourism is based, as the blue-collar masses seek to imitate the lives and tastes of the upper class, those "at the head of the social structure in point of reputability." Of course, he was referring to the fin de siècle grand tours of European capitals that the wealthy indulged in as a badge of status, the transatlantic whirlwind of cultural meccas later satirized by Mark Twain in *Innocents Abroad*. What neither Veblen nor Twain saw on the horizon was the trickle-down degradation of mass tourism: what was the chic destination for independent travelers a decade ago has been "discovered" and is today a burned out tourist trap. Hash-frayed Freak Street in Katmandu was replaced by Tibet, which is now overwhelmed by Chinese tourists, so now the cool place to head is to Bhutan or Ladak.

Everywhere tourists go eventually becomes Bourbon Street or Atlantic City.

Veblen brings up the categories of conspicuous consumption, vicarious consumption, conspicuous leisure, and conspicuous waste as the most telling emblems of leisure class activities. These are now the main selling points of what we call the "hospitality industry." With factory-like repetition, their job is to market well branded travel routes to less sophisticated travelers. We first see travel consumerism on screen in Jacques Tati's 1967 film *Playtime*. In this wicked satire, the beleaguered Parisian Monsieur Hulot stumbles through an occupying army of Ugly Americans carted around in tour buses, their adenoidal Midwestern accents in shrill contrast to the murmured French of locals. Strategically, Tati created a set of plateglass highrises to represent Paris, one that resembles downtown Dallas, as if visitors were being shown a place they'd recognize as home. The real Paris appears only for a fleeting moment as Notre Dame is reflected in a tour bus window and a lone vendor sells flowers at her funky corner kiosk. Meanwhile, the women tourists chatter about their lives back home against a glossy backdrop of what they think is the City of Lights.

Needless to say, I seldom travel anymore except to visit with friends in my old haunts of San Francisco, New York, Madrid,

Barcelona, and Florida. I never stay in hotels, see the sites, or eat in trendy new restaurants and do exactly what I'd be doing if I still lived there. Actually, it's more time travel than geographical. Yet I still need to pop a Xanax to survive the airports and flights that bring me there. Last April I found what I thought was a great round-trip deal from New Orleans to Madrid on Norwegian Air, then later questioned my very sanity as I endured a Southwest flight to Los Angeles just to catch a nonstop to Madrid. On the return flight, I was stuck in airports in Madrid, London, and Orlando for fifty-two hours due to unconscionable delays on the part of Norwegian, which operates with shocking inefficiency for a Scandinavian company. To get me through my next descent into airport hell, make that dose of Xanax a double.

For years now, I immediately start sneezing the minute I board a plane, and my sniffling and sporadic *achoos* continue throughout the flight. In these days of coronavirus panic, I'd be escorted off the plane. There must be some allergen in the air-recycling filter that sets off my childhood hay fever, now only triggered by springtime live oak pollen. And I often come down with a mild grippe or slight cold after a flight.

Which is why, if I were a virus, mass tourism is exactly how I'd choose to conquer the world.

The path the virus took from Wuhan in December to New Orleans in March is clearly delineated. During the customary travel of the two-week Chinese New Year holiday, which this Year of the Metal Rat began on January 24, 430,000 Chinese flew into the United States, at least 40,000 of whom landed in New York. The next month, during the Carnival weekend of February 20, more than a million tourists descended on New Orleans to celebrate Mardi Gras. This street celebration is a shoulder-to-shoulder hoedown, the polar opposite of social distancing. A recent *New York Times* article connected the coronavirus outbreak in New Orleans to New York City with genome sequencing. Based on eighty-nine samples, this analysis traced 100 percent of the New Orleans infections back to New York. Contrary to a once-proposed theory, this year's New Orleans Carnival didn't cause a boom in infections in other parts of the country. In Louisiana, the genome branches of infection are short and disappear. In other words, the disease came from elsewhere and stayed here. Already infected asymptomatic tourists, including those who first contracted the virus in jam-packed airports and planes, arrived on the crowded streets, had a great time, then retuned to New York before falling ill themselves, leaving 468 people to later die in New Orleans.

"Throw me something, mister," parade watchers shout to the masked float riders tossing plastic beads and trinkets—all made in China, of course—into the crowds. This year the masked locals may have been generous with their throws, but they themselves caught something else made in China along the parade routes.

Travel bans are now in place between most countries and even between certain states. Airlines are running at 3 percent of their capacity, and most international flights have been canceled. The steroidal hospitality industry may never recover the public trust it once had, and now that it's been proven potentially lethal, perhaps it shouldn't. As a twenty-year resident of the French Quarter as well as an eight-year resident of Barcelona's Barrio Gótico, squeezed out of both of those neighborhoods that I once called home by the mushrooming of other people's leisure travel, I'm not sad to see it go. I used to walk those familiar streets, greeting passing friends every few blocks, but now as I wedge my way through the surf of ogling strangers, cell phone maps aglow, there's nobody with whom I care to speak.

I figure their lives must be pretty boring to come all this way to stare at mine.

16

Here are a few of the baffling mixed messages about the coronavirus that we've received during the past two months of spring, 2020:

Then: Cotton face masks are unnecessary and don't protect anyone from the expelled aerosolized particulates of the virus. *Now*: Facemasks are essential when leaving home, and their use in public is mandatory in certain cities, as well as when shopping or riding public transit in most places.

Then: The virus doesn't thrive in hot, humid weather. *Now*: Two of the hardest hit hotspots are sultry New Orleans and southeast Louisiana, along with tropical Brazil.

Then: Many Black people believed themselves protected from contagion by the melanin in their skin. *Now*: In Louisiana, 70 percent of the coronavirus deaths have occurred among Blacks.

Then: Young adults are immune. *Now*: There's an alarming spike of twenty- and thirty-year-olds dying of strokes caused by virus-related blood clots.

Then: Check in on the elderly with frequent care visits. *Now*: Don't go anywhere near seniors, destined to die isolated in nursing homes, where nationwide a third of the coronavirus deaths have occurred.

Then: The major symptoms of infection are a high fever, shortness of breath, and a persistent dry cough. *Now*: Many admitted to ICUs with coronavirus are experiencing severe fatigue, diarrhea, and intestinal ailments as their primary ailments.

Then: The virus settles in the lungs. *Now*: The cornavirus attacks the heart, kidneys, and brain.

Then: It's so easy and convenient to work from home with videoconferencing and Zoom. *Now*: "Your voice cut off again. I can't figure out how to control this damn thing. This is driving me crazy and sucking up all my time. My internet surges in and out after the latest rainstorm brought down my connection for three days."

Then: Smoking is among the most severe risk factors for the infection. *Now*: French doctors are putting nicotine patches on the virus patients in their hospitals and theorize that smoking may somehow prevent coronavirus.

Then: Animals can't contract the virus. *Now*: Several tigers and lions in zoos have tested positive, as well as various dogs and cats. Evidently these animals were infected by zookeepers or pet owners. Can infected pets pass on the virus to humans? Should they be fitted with snug face masks? Stay tuned.

Then: Children don't contract the coronavirus. *Now*: Several children infected with the virus are developing a life-threatening inflammatory overreaction of the immune system in fighting it.

Then: After a few thousands deaths, the pandemic will be kaput by summer. *Now*: Approximately a million Americans could die of coronavirus, infections will peak again this fall, and the pandemic will continue until a vaccine is available in 2022.

Then: Just stay home and you'll be safe. *Now*: Microwave your mail before opening it, disinfect surfaces in your house every three hours, wipe off doorknobs with hand sanitizer, insist deliveries be left at the front door, and freak out with a behavior so manic that previously you'd have been diagnosed with obsessive-compulsive disorder.

17

Today I received word that my close friend Pilar, a renowned Spanish translator, died in Madrid on Sunday. When I stayed with Pilar and her husband Esteban last spring, she seemed as vital and expansive as ever, although she was undergoing chemotherapy for metastasized breast cancer. Evidently her condition worsened this January, when she started receiving radiation, but that abruptly stopped in March when Madrid went into full lockdown, the epicenter of the coronavirus pandemic in Spain. In the hospitals, hundreds were dying daily of the virus, so many that their cadavers were stored in an enormous ice-skating rink called the Palacio de Hielo.

I spoke with Esteban three weeks ago, and he explained that Pilar's stark choice was either to continue her treatment at the hospital, where she might become infected with the cornonavirus and then would have to die alone, or to pass away of cancer at home. As I would have, she chose the latter and died in her own bed with peace and dignity, surrounded by family. Recently thousands of people have made the same decision, to die of urgent medical conditions at home rather than endure the forced isolation of a pandemic hospital.

Pilar never had coronavirus, but should also be counted as one of its victims.

The last time I saw her was this past April. Stalwart friends, both she and Esteban had risen at six a.m. to see me off on my ill-fated return flight on Norwegian Air that stranded me in airports for two days. This being Madrid, we'd returned home at three that morning from a jovial goodbye dinner at some friends' house, and I'd stayed up slugging back cognacs and packing. A pale presence in her bathrobe, Pilar drifted in to sit with me at the dining room table as I gulped coffee, trying to reeve up energy for the airport marathon ahead.

"You're a tower of strength, Pilar," I told her. "You'll make it."

She gave me one of her throaty baritone laughs. "If you say so."

"How many more months of chemo?" I asked. "What do the doctors say?"

Observing Spanish formality about private matters, we'd never before discussed her medical condition, although we'd roared our way through every other topic in the lexicon.

"I don't have much faith left in what doctors tell me," she confessed, leaning across the table. "Not many know this, but when I was in my forties my doctor advised me to take estrogen replacement therapy to slow the effects of menopause, and that's what caused this cancer." She pulled the lapels of her bathrobe closed, as if she'd exposed too much of her feminine vanity. "Why should I listen to doctors now?"

"I know, like they recommend testosterone treatments for us aging men, which causes prostate cancer. I'm not buying it."

"I did."

That was our last conversation before I jumped in a taxi to Barajas airport. Pilar had revealed to me her deepest secret: trusting doctors to preserve youth. At first I didn't understand why she felt compelled to tell me that during the final moments we spent together, nine months before the pandemic exploded, hunched over a table in the hazy gray dawn of a spring day. But now I do. So I'd understand the choice she finally made to die in her own bed at home, far from the dinging alarms and wincing fluorescent lights of a hospital, where once again she'd have to trust the judgment of doctors.

Pilar is a common name for Spanish women, who are literally the pillars of strength in their culture. Ironically, Madrid was seeded with the coronavirus this year on March 8, during a demonstration to celebrate International Women's Day, to which 120,000 Spaniards flocked. On that same day, the March issue of the prestigious Spanish magazine *Revista de Occidente*, published by the Ortega y Gasset Foundation, arrived at news kiosks. My essay in that issue, titled "How Do You Pronounce Latinx?: Sexual Harassment, the Puritan Pillory, and Gender Ideology," had been commissioned by another close friend, a married lesbian and feminist scholar María Luisa Maillard, who edited this special edition devoted to women. I suspected that my essay, wryly critical of gender ideology and its distortions of language, along with the excesses of the "MeToo" movement, might raise the hackles of some doctrinaire feminist readers, but then again, I'm never convinced that I've written anything significant unless it offends somebody, somewhere. I was prepared for some blowback, if not to be confined to a Puritan pillory for heresy, but didn't expect half of Madrid to drop dead the day the issue hit the stands.

María Luisa emailed me today from a Madrid in tight lockdown: "The city hasn't gone into a Phase I reopening, so the restrictions haven't been relaxed. The management of the pandemic has been a disaster and we're deeply concerned about this notorious State of Emergency. We've lost all of our rights." She knows of what she speaks, after having spent the first twenty years of her life under a Fascist dictatorship in Franco's Spain. She has cause to be worried after growing up with such rigid controls as a child and young woman.

Here the city is preparing a Phase I reopening this Saturday, May 16, the terms of which remain heavy-handed and confusing. Restaurants may use 25 percent of their dining space to seat socially distanced customers, who must first make a reservation then register their names and contact information for tracing purposes should a fellow diner later be identified as infected. Franco would have loved this restaurant registration policy to track where conspiring Communists from the underground resistance dined. My gym will reopen in two weeks, but the city health department will keep off-limits not only the swimming pool, steam room, and sauna, the only facilities I use, but the showers and locker rooms. We are told to wear face masks in public, to maintain this distancing rigmarole, and to follow government and medical guidelines.

If I'd always followed government mandates, I'd have been killed in Vietnam fifty years ago trying to defend American economic interests in Southeast Asia by stopping the so-called "domino effect" spread of Chinese Communism. Instead I became a fervent draft resister. If I'd always complied with medical counsel, as a nineteen-year-old I would have been confined to a ward for adolescent schizophrenics for two years and subjected to electroshock treatments. You see, my parents and I had a bit of a disagreement about how I was launching my life as a young poet, so at that age they had me committed for several months to a mental hospital that wanted to keep me locked up for extended therapy. Instead, I bolted.

In the first case, for the good of my country, I was told. And in the second, for my own health.

My distrust of government and medical authority runs long and deep.

18

It's confirmed: a neighbor two stories below has been keeping a caged duck with clipped wings named Ruthie, after the famed French Quarter character Ruthie the Duck Girl. The neighbor, with whom I haven't spoken before during the five years I've lived here, tells me that the duck is a wounded rescue animal she found in a City Park lagoon. For a while I was convinced that the quacking was the mating call of a menacing murder of crows I just noticed circling the sky at dusk every day.

Caw. Caw. Caw.

Other birds have returned—blue jays, mourning doves, and sparrows—and every evening, after the six o'clock Angelus chimes from the dome of Our Lady of the Holy Rosary church across the street, I sit on my balcony next to the three-hundred year-old oak tree to watch the birds, squirrels, owls, and possums that scamper through its branches. Since the pandemic began, global carbon dioxide emissions have declined 17 percent. With less petroleum exhaust and artificial lighting, nature has come surging back.

I wonder if the recent pandemics—HIV, SARS, avian influenza, swine flu, Zika, Ebola, and now the coronavirus—are nature's immune system responses sent out to attack the metastasizing cancer of human overdevelopment. Most of these viruses have their origins in animals, not that the monkeys, bats, chickens, pigs, and mosquitoes specifically are targeting us, but that nature as a self-contained biological organism has both a shared will and consciousness of its own, what the botanist Rupert Sheldrake calls "morphic resonance." We might compare it to a worldwide mycelium of subterranean forest fungi, a collective internet of interconnected organic life in constant communication and transformation. The virus of modern civilization threatens this self-regulating mycelium, and climate change caused by our pollution will soon have the natural world in its death throes. So why shouldn't nature defend itself from the human virus in the same way that our own bodies protect themselves from destructive pathogens?

When we get the flu, for instance, our bodies go into high alert, each part pitching in to ensure our survival. Fever causes us to sweat out infectious toxins, fatigue sends us to bed for restorative sleep, and sneezing and coughing empty our lungs of mucous. The nastiest symptoms of the flu are ways that the body employs to rid itself of the nefarious bug that threatens its very survival.

So maybe nature, in an automatic immunological response, is trying to cough, sneeze, broil, freeze, blow, flood, quake, and burn our encroaching civilization away, one human at a time. Lately our infectious presence is so threatening that it seems as if we're racing from one natural disaster to another.

In the scant seven-decade span of my own lifetime, the world population has almost tripled, now approaching eight billion people. In the surreal satirist William Burroughs's *Cities of the Red Night*, an uncannily prophetic novel published in 1981 about a pandemic ravaging the earth, a sinister Colonel Dimitri sums up the crisis to the global private eye, Sam Snide:

> Jerry was a carrier of the illness. He did not die of it directly. Winkler, who was thirty years older, died in a few days. Well . . . there are those who think a selective pestilence is the most humane solution to overpopulation and the attendant impasses of pollution, inflation, and exhaustion of natural resources. A plague that kills the old and leaves the young, minus a reasonable percentage . . . one might be tempted to let such an epidemic run its course even if one had the power to stop it.

Dimitri points out that a virus is literally a copy, as is our human DNA. "Changes, Mr. Snide, can only be effected by alterations in the *original.*" A pandemic, in which infectious copies are invading genetic copies in a battle for survival, could be a sign that we have replicated our species into extinction. To nature, humans are the virus, and according to Dimitri, "they will multiply their assholes into the polluted seas."

This evening, during the first week in May, Formosan termites are starting to swarm around streetlights and lit windows. Much like the virus imported from Wuhan that plagues us now, this highly destructive species is an invasive one that arrived here during the forties from Taiwan. These wood-pulverizing insects usually swarm, mate, and build new hives in May, and a termite infestation can reduce wooden structures, banisters, and support beams to marshmallow in a matter of months. It's curious that, attracted by light, the insects are crawling all over the balcony table where I've strung a single line of electric lights, a sign of human habitation, but ignore the solar lights lining the rest of the balcony, as if only man-made energy holds any promise of their further propagation. These destructive termites remind me that hurricane season along the Gulf Coast begins in a month. Coronavirus, termites, and now hurricanes: is vengeful nature hitting us this year with a one-two-three punch?

We read in the Old Testament of plagues, locust swarms, and floods sent by Jehovah to wipe out corrupt regimes and cruel leaders. Perhaps the prophets who wrote those pages intuited a God that acts much like the immunological system of nature. At the moment, even as the coronavirus spikes, the biblical locusts are swarming in Africa, devouring every crop in their path. What is nature trying to tell us? Although this evening the birds and other creatures in the live oak branches assure me that nature is in a constant state of bountiful renewal, the pandemic also indicates that it's threatened, pissed off at us, and fighting back.

My only solace during these lockdown days, when I often feel like a fat, lazy housecat, is to drink a glass of wine at sunset on the balcony, seated at the round, glass tabletop under the live oak tree towering above me, its twisted branches extending over four neighboring backyards. Now more than ever this enormous tree has become the totem spirit that shields me from both the merciless Louisiana sun above and the pandemic outside. Trees think in longer terms than we do. Until the sixties, live oak limbs in this neighborhood where I grew up were draped with gray beards of Spanish moss, as they still are in nearby City Park. But decades ago unrelenting car pollution put an end to those hazy silhouettes of moss.

Covered with bark as gnarled as the resilient old man I've become, this overarching live oak contains my spirit in its expansive limbs. It keeps me alive. Reminds me of those I've loved and lost through the three epidemics I've survived, and I wonder how long I can sit here at a social distance like this tree, solitary and self-contained. The final lines of Walt Whitman's "I Saw in Louisiana a Live-Oak Growing" come to mind, the perfect words with which to close this lockdown before a new reopening is upon us, together with whatever that may bring:

> . . . and though the live-oak glistens there in Louisiana
> solitary in wide flat space,
> Uttering joyous leaves all its life without a friend a lover near,
> I know very well I could not.

Part II

The Opening

A plague o' both your houses!
—Shakespeare, *Romeo and Juliet*

1

The closing was a snap compared to the opening. The so-called New Normal has proven to be one irritation after another, either from a jittery fear of infection by the coronavirus or the often irrational rules put in place to prevent that from happening.

During the apparent height of the pandemic, most of us just stayed home. Now going out involves as many restrictive protocols as being screened by border guards when crossing into an enemy country. After two months of quarantine, when most people in New Orleans should either be healthy, recovered, or already dead, suddenly face masks are required to enter my neighborhood grocery. Yet during the past two feverish months of self-isolation amid spiking death rates, masks were optional. Talk about closing the barn door after the horse has bolted.

By order of the mayor, shop owners who don't require customers to wear masks can be fined. Mayor LaToya Cantrell (who I call LaToyota Can't Tell) is coming down hard in her Phase I reopening requirements, much stricter than the governor's guidelines for the rest of the state. This may be because at one time New Orleans reported one of the highest death rates in the country. Either that, or to make skittish people feel more secure about going out in public, whether they actually are safer or not.

What I suspect is that these more draconian rules are the mayor's attempt to beef up her laissez-faire image after being lambasted nationally for not canceling the deadly Mardi Gras that contaminated the city. Locally her administration is seen as a failing one, a coronavirus hotspot with scant public testing in a city impoverished by massive unemployment from the collapsed tourism industry. The bald truth is that 40 percent of the deaths in Louisiana have occurred inside nursing homes. In many other states, this is where more than half of the total fatalities have taken place. In Pennsylvania, nursing homes account for 69 percent of the dead. I'm certain that those tragic elderly residents, trapped in virus incubators and isolated even from family members, never once set foot in anybody's neighborhood groceries and pharmacies.

So why face masks, and why now?

Their main effect seems to be as a patriotic social prop, not as a medical precaution. They've become emblems of solidarity, as after 9/11 when many Americans sported flag pins, which, of course, did nothing to prevent international terrorism. Whether to wear those pins occasionally flared into heated discussions, most reflecting an opinion of President George W. Bush, who spearheaded their popularity. In the same way, the simmering face mask civil war often seems based on feelings about Donald Trump, who refuses to wear such a mask. This week two friends called to rant against those selfish folks who won't wear face masks in public. They cited a wide variety of statistics—30 percent, 50 percent, 70 percent effective—gleaned from God knows where. I sidestepped their hotheaded diatribes by asking if we could politely agree to disagree, understanding how easily fear can flip into anger, terror into rage.

Even though I sympathize with these friends' craving for security, illusionary as it might be, I find the masks filthy, asphyxiating, and inconvenient and have read scant evidence proving that they prevent contagion. In Iceland, a small, sensible country that has eliminated the virus through rigorous testing and tracing, "masks aren't even part of the public conversation," according to a recent article in the *New Yorker*. The country's health director, Alma Möller, in charge of Iceland's response to the pandemic, claims that "wearing one might be advisable for a person who is sick and coughing, but that person shouldn't be walking around in public anyway. 'We think they don't add much and they can give a false sense of security,' she said. 'Also, masks work for some time, and then they get wet, and don't work anymore." New Orleans writer and epidemiologist John Barry commented in a recent radio interview that a face mask blocks the tiny aerosolized particulates in breath as ineffectively as a chain-link fence would stop a mosquito, although he agrees with Möller that a mask worn by someone with a hacking cough would obstruct a spew of particulates closer to the size of a baseball.

Basically, I comply when required, much as I would at a beach-front shop with a "no shoes, no service" sign. Yet my face mask is the filthiest thing I've ever put on my body except for the jockstrap I was forced to wear during high school gym class. For years it was stuffed at the bottom of my gym bag because I was too embarrassed to hand it over to my grandmother to wash and then line dry in the backyard, in full view of the neighbors. I soon learned that my crotch rot wasn't called jock itch for nothing and recently have spotted ads to cure fungal eruptions of facial jock itch caused by wearing face masks.

On Saturday, May 16, the first day of the much-heralded re-opening, I needed yogurt, kale salad, and wine. Entering the grocery, all I had at the time was a black paisley scarf to tie around my nose and mouth, a dressy silk one that matched my black T-shirt and cargo shorts. I felt like quite the plague fashionplate. My glasses immediately fogged, but gripping my hand basket, I stumbled through the suffocating experience, yanking off the sweaty scarf the minute I stepped outside.

Two days ago the armed security guard, a heavyset, mocha-skinned woman who seldom budges from her swiveling bar chair stationed near the door, handed me the free face mask I now use, of the one-ply cotton variety. We'd only had one previous encounter. In March she'd barked at me like a prison guard about a new store policy that required using the handsanitizer dispenser at the door. I swept past her, not sure what she was mouthing under her mask. She raced down the aisle after me and—ignoring social distancing, I might add—got right in my face.

"The freaking rule is for your own damn safety," she screamed.

That was the only moment during the pandemic when I've lost it, shouting back that I refused to do anything against my will supposedly for my own good. "My own good as determined by whom?" I demanded.

As Camus points out in his novel, plagues tend to bring out both the best and worst in human nature. The best is the angelic devotion of those in direct contact with human suffering, personified in the novel by Dr. Rieux, one of those dedicated doctors and nurses who care for the sick and dying. The worst is in the rest of us observing from the sidelines, far removed from the agonies of the afflicted. In people like us, plagues spark either a contagion of paralyzing terror or petty rebellions against the often-futile restrictions used to control them.

At that moment, the pandemic was bringing out the worst in me, and I was getting a glimpse of the snarling imp of the perverse buried deep inside. Not a pretty sight. After all, the guard was just doing her underpaid job, dealing with this Rumpelstiltskin tantrum of an older man in the only way she knew how, as if he were her unruly grandbaby. The guard and I drew a small crowd along with the furious manager, a usually affable, ruddy-cheeked guy born in the then Soviet-controlled Ukraine.

"While on private property," he shouted, face flushing even redder, "you have to obey the rules or shop elsewhere."

Which I did for a while. On my next visit to that grocery, a Post-it note was stuck to that life-saving Purell dispenser: "Out." The next time I entered there was another scrawled note: "Out of Order." Then the dispenser disappeared for good, along with that fly-by-night regulation to assure my own safety. So much for essential public health measures. These days the hand sanitizer enforcer patrols social distancing in the checkout line, when not seated at the door immersed in her cell phone screen, the principal focus of her tedious days. And wearing my new face mask, we now nod at each other in complicit exasperation, rolling our eyes as if to ask each other *when will this bullshit be over?*

2

Today I received a note letter-headed "The White House, Washington," signed by President Donald J. Trump. It announces the stale news that "Your Economic Impact Payment Has Arrived," meaning the check I received two weeks ago. "As we wage total war on this invisible enemy, we are working around the clock . . . America will triumph yet again—and rise to new heights of greatness." I suspect Trump penned this inane prose himself, or the rhetoric was lifted from one of his press briefings: *total war, invisible enemy, make America great again.*

This week he announced that he's taking daily doses of the anti-malarial drug hydroxychloroquine to ward off the coronavirus, a pharmaceutical unproven to have any effect on either contagion or infection. I'm familiar with harmless quinine, of which I popped a daily dose to ward off malaria during my many months traveling in India. But mosquito-transmitted malaria has nothing to do with this strain of the SARS virus. This quinine-based chemical variant has been confirmed to provoke dangerous cardiovascular side effects in certain people. Especially, as the Speaker of the House was quick to point out, in the "morbidly obese," a testy jab at the fatso in the White House. This is the lofty level of discourse that has been trumpeted during the 2020 presidential campaign.

Now we have not only bread and circuses, but—presto!—a magic cure. Trump has moved into full P.T. Barnum mode, not only with giveaways and dancing elephants, but with a sure-fire snake-oil straight from a traveling medicine show. What many don't fathom about Donald Trump's wide popular appeal is that he's the contemporary incarnation of a deeply rooted American archetype—the nineteenth-century huckster, those garish, strike-it-rich tricksters who helped to settle the West while fleecing everyone in sight before moving on to the next frontier town. Of course, Twitter is his own version of standing on a barrelhead to address a circle of wide-eyed suckers.

Meanwhile Joe Biden, whose most appealing attribute is level-headed human warmth, remains in full lockdown, campaigning by podcast from his basement. This extreme political polarization running parallel to the pandemic panic has produced what to my mind is the most alarmingly weird era I've ever lived through in American history. And as if my seventy-odd years aren't enough, an eighty-seven year-old writer friend agrees with me. She's not exactly thrilled to have lived this long to experience what's happening in 2020.

Back when I was in Sunday school Bible class in 1957, as we paged through the Apostle John's Book of Revelation, my ten-year-old mind not only struggled to grasp the mysterious apocalyptic visions of the New Testament prophet but also the dizzying dimensions of a time that stretched so far into the future. And I remember that the most distant date I could conjure was precisely 2020. Perhaps it was the magical symmetry of the number or the vertiginous dive into a sci-fi odyssey—sixty-two light-years away!—that it entailed. At that point I guessed that anyone over fifteen was at least a hundred, so little did I understand aging and the passing of time.

And now that I'm alive in the year 2020, the cliff over which my childhood imagination dared not peek, it does seem like the dropping-off point of a once familiar world, one without any discernible connection to the past or resonance with a recognizable future. At this point life can seem much like the scenarios that John of Patmos prophesized, filled with seven-headed beasts, spirits foul as frogs, and a blasphemous harlot decked out in the plague color palette: "The woman was arrayed in purple and scarlet . . . holding in her hand a golden cup full of abominations . . . so shall her plagues come in a single day, pestilence and mourning and famine, and she shall be burned with fire." Revelation ends with the dire warning not to invent any more punitive visions: "if anyone adds to them, God will add to him the plagues described in this book."

May we add to the list of abominations a morbidly obese orange beast with a dyed comb-over, social distancing squares marked on sidewalks, and an incipient civil war over wearing face masks, not to mention the purple-and-scarlet vampire whores of that "invisible enemy," the coroanavirus pandemic? My ten-year-old self doubted that any of St. John's hallucinatory visions could ever come true, even on the barely imaginable horizon of 2020.

Yet here we are during the opening, waiting for what John calls "a new heaven and a new earth."

3

A fleeting glimpse of the old heaven on earth occurred just yesterday evening as once again I was taking my daily walk to the grocery. I heard somebody strumming a stirring flamenco guitar from across Esplanade Avenue in front of the Spanish restaurant Lola's, which was founded by my Andalusian friend Angel González, who passed away a decade ago.

Could it possibly be John Lawrence, I wondered, the guitarist with whom I'd collaborated for years at various flamenco tablaos, reciting García Lorca while John played and dancers stomped, clapped *palmas*, and clacked their castanets?

Who else could it be?

I crossed the street, and the guitarist was not only John but there was Lale, Angel's flamenco-dancer wife. She was stomping out an *alegria* rhythm in tennis shoes on the sidewalk together with another dancer, Micaela, flashing a perfect *seguiria* profile as she swooped along beside her.

In the middle of this Phase I opening, I'd stumbled upon an impromptu sidewalk flamenco tablao filled with old friends glowing like Blakean angels. We hugged and kissed unapologetically, while waiters wearing face masks served paellas to the outdoor tables in front of the restaurant. Bottles of Rioja appeared at our own table, and we caught up: Lale's operation in locked-down Houston, John's new carpentry gig, Micaela's videoed ballet classes from New York, my new book. John's wife, a Brazilian named Nubia, reported that her parents, who live right next door to them, had been stuck in Brazil for months, where they'd gone to visit family and now weren't allowed to fly back into the United States. We heard that another friend, a local poet in lockdown, was recovering from the searing indignity of watching her own mother's funeral in North Carolina on Zoom. Inside the church, her extensive family was represented by only the requisite ten mourners.

A police car mounted with a flashing blue light pulled up in front of the restaurant, and I held my breath. In a flashback to Fascist Spain, I thought that here come the *guardias civiles*. Then the cop car moved on, perhaps to a real crime scene where somebody was being shot.

I remembered this distant life—friends, live music, dancing, hugging—as if it were yesterday. Because, in fact, it was just yesterday, or three apocalyptic months ago, and now I couldn't believe what I'd been missing.

Then thunder clapped and torrential sheets of rain poured down, and this long-lost life I'd rediscovered disappeared before my eyes in a heartbeat. We couldn't regroup inside the restaurant itself, already filled to its 25 percent seating limit, so we dispersed. And suddenly the evening found me alone again, face mask dangling from one ear, waiting under the grocery awning with a half-gallon of milk in my shopping bag, staring at the pellets of downpour bouncing off the tarmac of the empty street as I wondered where the magic had gone.

Then I shuffled home to lockdown in the drizzle.

4

Yesterday I was relieved that the bank lobby I entered was at least open, but the personal bankers' cubicles were empty, and only a few employees were cowering inside a floor-to-ceiling plastic cage surrounding the tellers' stations. Phone calls to the bank had turned into endless dialogues with robot voices, so there I was to open a new savings account in person. I finally caught the attention of one banker, who curtly informed me that to transact any business I would need to bring in my "personal devices," which sounded a bit kinky.

Trying to close a matured CD last week from a bank in Massachusetts, after myriad calls to the branch I finally reached the genial manager quarantined at home in his attic, who arranged the direct deposit of my funds while enthusing about his garden. A personal phone call cuts through reams of red tape, avoiding the endless hours of online typing that I've come to dread. Dealing with a local bank has proven much thornier. The manager is only available by phone for two hours during the early morning, the lobby is closed, and any transaction involves filling out, notarizing, and scanning byzantine forms or driving deep into the burbs to shout through a microphone at a drive-through teller.

Now that we're allowed to take care of business again, any attempt turns into a full-time job. The customer is forced to accomplish online the tasks of those employees "working from home." Convenient downtown branches remain mysteriously shuttered, lobbies are vacant, phones are answered by robots that drone on with boilerplate messages in English and Spanish, and should you be lucky enough to catch an actual employee to speak to through a face mask and plexiglass screen, information is spotty and unhelpful. Conversations are testy, regulations change haphazardly from one day to the next, and nobody knows what the new rules are.

I really need a hair cut, so I sat wide-eyed reading the emailed reopening instructions from my French Quarter hair salon. Mickey, my Cajun hairdresser, is an animated one-man show, drawing everyone inside his cramped shop into the entertaining banter he maintains over blaring pop music. He's flexible about scheduling as well as keeping appointments, and while waiting I don't mind flipping through magazines I'd otherwise never read. Now customers must (1) stand outside in the sweltering heat of a New Orleans summer until the previous client has exited the shop; (2) undergo a temperature check before entering; (3) use hand sanitizer on arrival and departure; (4) maintain social distancing as one of only two customers and hairdressers allowed inside at a time; and (5) wear a face mask. How do you maintain distance while someone is washing and cutting your hair? What if the face mask gets soggy during the shampoo, or after waiting outside on the hot sidewalk, you enter in a sweat that makes the thermometer gun pointed at your forehead ding?

To avoid this ordeal, I've decided to grow a pandemic ponytail.

I hope that the Center for Disease Control has managed to save at least a few people with the convoluted rules that are making our lives unbearable. To the point where I dread doing anything more complicated than buying a baguette. Public health officials, no matter how correct they may be, can't reorganize a bustling civic democracy in the same lockstep way in which they'd restructure a threatened hospital or military camp. No nurses or sergeants are present at every turn shouting orders to assure that procedures are correctly carried out. Fines, mandates, and ordinances lack any authority, because we didn't elect the people responsible for them. In spite of the "invisible enemy" of the pandemic, most of us haven't signed up to be obedient foot soldiers. Nobody seems to be in charge. We're blindly following the orders of people following orders who are oblivious to their immediate consequences in our daily lives.

"Distancing" itself is a precarious basis for reorganization, since most aspects of business and life thrive on the proximity of personal contact. With all of these stuttering phases of reopening, the sheer terror these new rules are striking in the hearts of many frightened Americans may last a lifetime.

"Feeling safe" is a highly subjective emotion. So is "going crazy."

And what makes some people feel safe makes others go crazy.

5

I've been wondering when people would flee their confinement and run screaming into the streets. I've been waiting for this quarantined country to explode, for fear to flip into its emotional twin, anger. Yet I never quite imagined the apocalyptic fires and smoke now spiraling through the midnight skies of so many American cities. And in my wildest dreams never pictured shop windows shattered by looters wearing pandemic face masks.

How long does it take for cooped up, stressed out, and unemployed people to riot? Like coronavirus victims gasping for air, for several months now many others haven't been able to breath. If there are any narratives older in human history than plagues, they are racism, tribal warfare, and the abuse of power. George Floyd's brutal murder by the police on Memorial Day in Minneapolis may have sparked the current protest marches, but what has fueled the arsons, looting, and street fighting has been a long-simmering reaction against the escalating militarization of the police presence in this country. This threat has been felt most severely in Black and Hispanic communities, but other groups have recently jumped into the fray to make their voices heard, including hotheaded right- and left-wing extremists.

What we learned in 2015 during the protests against the police murder of Michael Brown was that Ferguson, Missouri, and Fallujah, Iraq, had a lot in common: both were filled with US Army surplus, including mine-resistant armored protection vehicles (MRAPs), noise-based crowd control devices, M4 rifles, rubber bullets, and tear gas. The Department of Defense has either given or sold at bargain prices war equipment to local police. Eighty percent of small towns have military-style SWAT teams, as well as 90 percent of large cities. The result is that local cops, those once-helpful folks who used to walk their beats on flat feet swinging billy clubs to preserve civic order, are now trained to treat suspicious citizens like enemy insurgents in a war zone. I remember well the mounting anger and frustration we felt in the post-Katrina era in New Orleans during the prolonged military occupation of our devastated city by the National Guard. We, the few remaining people, were the enemy, or at least were treated as if we were.

And the message that we, the people, have sent during this past month is that both health and police authorities are choking us to death with public safety. George Floyd's dying words have become a protest mantra for a suffocating nation: "I can't breath." This happens to be the principal symptom for victims of the coranavirus. To our country's shame, an endless number of unarmed Black people have been killed by heavy-handed rogue cops, treating them not as potential lawbreakers but as if they were enemy terrorists. Of course, this goes as far back in history as you care to look. Yet not since the assassination of Martin Luther King in 1968 has there been such an explosive national protest.

The question remains: why now? This type of racist policing has been part of American history for centuries. Was it the modern technology of the cell phone videotape that finally proved it? Is this a long-delayed spring break for young people yanked out of school, jobs, and social life and quarantined inside during the past three months? Or as past plague narratives illustrate, is this yet another aspect of the inevitable social upheaval that accompanies most pandemics?

The actual details of the tragic story that triggered this chaos have yet to emerge. It seems that George Floyd, a Black man, bought a pack of menthol cigarettes from a convenience store with a counterfeit twenty-dollar bill. When the shop clerk noticed that the ink was still wet on the fake banknote, he went outside to Floyd's car to demand the cigarettes back, only to be rebuffed by a customer whom he described as drunk and disorderly. He called the police, and one of the four who arrived was Derek Chauvin, a White cop who had seventeen dismissed misconduct charges against him. Chauvin moonlighted as a guard at a Latino nightclub, El Nuevo Rodeo, where Floyd also worked as a bouncer. The cop handcuffed his fellow security worker, with whom he'd had repeated conflicts on the job, and pushed him into his squad car. Then—here the mystery remains—for some reason pulled him back out, threw him to the ground, and despite gasping protests that he couldn't breath, kneeled on his neck for more than nine minutes until he choked to death. Although there's been is no evidence that, as the clerk maintained, Floyd was either drunk or disorderly, an autopsy revealed an alarming mixture of fentanyl and methamphetamine in his system and that he was infected with the coronavirus. What he needed was a doctor and a drug counselor, not a cop with a personal vendetta against him.

"The situation in Minneapolis is no longer in any way about the murder of George Floyd," declared Tim Walz, governor of Minnesota. "It's about attacking civil society, instilling fear and disrupting out great cities." He claims that 80 percent of the rioters have come from out of state. This includes members of such Far Right fringe groups as Boogaloo Bois and the Three Percenters, dedicated to accelerating a White supremacist civil war in the United States. Other rioters such as Antifas and the Black Bloc represent the anarchist Left, who have long provoked violent confrontations with the police at orderly demonstrations.

Reports have surfaced of some Far Right rioters masquerading as Antifas, and perhaps the opposite is also true. Both groups are composed of young White men who probably have a lot in common. Frankly, I don't understand their parallel but polarized extremist violence. I suspect they're all members of the angry White ex-working class, underemployed survivors of stagnant regions such as the Rust Belt who feel marginalized from the mainstream. Lonely website junkies, they are delirious with dreams of glorious real-life action.

In some twisted way, their motives seem to align with the leftist Occupy Wall Street movement of several years ago as part of the class warfare against the super-wealthy 1 percent. The shops looted on Rodeo Drive in Beverly Hills and in uptown Manhattan have been those that sell expensive items such as electronics, perfume, and jewelry. In other words, these aren't hungry pandemic survivors grabbing food or other essentials, but people striking out at those who can afford to buy so much more. In a historical parallel, Daniel Defoe comments in *A Journal of the Plague Year* that the stubborn persistence of the pestilence in London during 1665 also threw into sharp contrast what he calls the "voluptuousness" in which the rich luxuriated while self-quarantined inside their houses, with a general lawlessness of the less fortunate on the street. "Rioters abounded," he observes, "as did thieves and lunatics."

Far from protesting against racism, many of these lunatic extremists seem dedicated to fomenting a war between law enforcement and American citizens during which the police can use their scary new military equipment against the rest of us. The technique these groups have employed in Minneapolis, New York, St. Louis, and many other cities is to use the ranks of the peaceful Black Lives Matter protestors as a safety shield, launching out to commit acts of vandalism, and then melting back into the chanting crowds. Whether they were legitimate protestors or out-of-town instigators, in forty-three American cities more than 13,500 people have been arrested, only to be crammed inside the same jails that public health authorities have been trying to empty to stop the spread of the coronavirus.

Forget the Phase I, Phase II, and Phase III reopening. With these urban guerrillas, the pandemic lockdown has broken wide open. Some may have been previous lockdown protestors, fed up with the painfully slow relaxation of pandemic restrictions. Many may wear face masks to avoid police surveillance cameras or teargas, not as a precaution against contagion. One thing is clear: rioters don't socially distance. Overnight, city streets have been transformed from deserted corridors of lurking infection to swarming combat zones of fire, rubber bullets, tear gas, and lunging masses of people, some of them armed. Ignoring curfews, the hate-filled fringes have united in sowing collective mayhem.

Take, for instance, the Boogaloo Bois—a frenchified misspelling of "boys," with no reference to Blanche or any other Bois—who refer to their anticipated racial civil war as the Big Boogaloo. That they'd turn up armed at Black Lives Matter demonstrations in their trademark Hawaiian shirts just to kick up the dust means that they've learned how to eat Jim Crow, so to speak, and take second billing. They co-starred in the Unite the Right rally three years ago in Charlottesville, chanting "Jews will not replace us" as they pranced around in shorts carrying lit tiki torches as if they were at some fabulous gay patio party. They obviously feel that their manhood is under threat, either as macho Romeos, breadwinners, or supposedly superior White men. Many identify online as "incels," or celibates spurned by women.

I must say that if anyone thinks that they can make this rambunctiously adolescent pioneer country march in a civilized lockstep, whether for reasons of public health or social order, good luck. That schoolmarm Hillary Clinton tried it four years ago, and you can see the chaotic despot we've gotten in her place.

In spite of a criminal minority of trigger-happy bullies on far too many police forces, most of us reasonably sane and civilized

Americans believe in the slogan Black Lives Matter. Just as a majority of the French during the French Revolution supported the cause of *liberté, égalilté, et fraternité*. Those inspired idealists took to the streets in unruly mass demonstrations chanting these cherished concepts upon which our own democracy is based. Then aristocratic heads-rolled, the Bourbon dynasty was dethroned, the Bastille prison was stormed, mayhem erupted, and in contemporary terms, the police were defunded. Along with churches, the parochial institutions that sheltered the needy were shuttered, sending masses of the crippled, homeless, and deranged flooding into the streets. Sound familiar?

What soon followed was Robespierre's vengeful Reign of Terror to control the battling mobs of revolutionaries and counterrevolutionaries, during which those revolutionaries judged as politically incorrect were in the most literal sense canceled, not by public censure but by the guillotine. This incipient civil war was ended only by the rise of that populist imperialist, Napoleon Bonaparte, who proved that people prefer the iron hand of authoritarian rule to the violent chaos of polarized politics. I offer this oversimplified summary of late sixteenth-century French history only to point out the obvious parallels that alarm me now. The words may be inspiring and the causes just, but when offered the choice, people will always choose dictatorship over anarchy in the streets.

After all, we Vietnam War protestors swarming around police barricades in the sixties ended up with Richard Nixon, somewhat more of a gentleman than Donald Trump, although hardly as dashing as Napoleon.

6

"I'm doubtful," said the oldest member of my writing workshop when I asked if she'd participate in our resumed sessions this month.

"I understand." How else can I respond to upset people whose reasoning I can't quite follow?

First two members were on board, then four, and although they didn't represent the quorum I hoped for, I decided to continue anyway with the canceled spring semester of my independently-based writing workshop. The modest tuitions had been paid, and I couldn't afford to offer refunds. I'd telephoned each of the eight writers one by one rather than using a group email, thus avoiding a string of impulsively piggy-backed responses. While I can deal with an individual bee, I'd never stick my head inside a beehive, especially one of threatened bees. And I knew that after three months of quarantine, sitting together in a room might terrify certain people, and terror can be contagious. One member described what she called her "angst" at being together in a room with other people, so I began with a list of four confirmations, three Angsts, and one Doubtful.

The members had organized a weekly emotional support group on Zoom, which I never joined. And I declined to do online workshops, unable to imagine how I could conduct a detailed discussion of either a published literary text or a member's manuscript facing a computer screen. How do you flip to the first sentence in the third paragraph on page four while clicking? Perhaps I'm old-fashioned, but I believe that inspired teaching involves an ineffable interpersonal transfer of energy that requires face-to-face presence. My priest friend in northern California was asked by his parishioners to celebrate videoed Masses by propping a cell phone on the altar in his empty church. He also declined. "Without Communion," he told me, "there's no Mass, and I can't pass the host through a computer screen."

I feel the same way about teaching. In the best of cases, it's a communion of another sort, if not spiritual then intellectual and artistic, one that can't be transmitted through a computer screen.

Like my friend and neighbor Laura, several university and high school teacher friends forced to teach online complain that it sucks the very life out of them. They're oncall twelve to eighteen hours a day to answer students' emailed and phone queries to clarify doubts or misunderstandings. Laura confesses to hitting the booze much earlier in the day, long before cocktail hour. In fact, among those now working from home, the average American starts drinking at 4:36 p.m. These teachers tell me that half of their students drift in and out of the courses, and the others' work is difficult to evaluate. A lot of subtle engagement is communicated by body language, facial gestures, and direct eye contact. This is what office hours and after-class conversations are about: a certain twinkle in the eye that ignites a reciprocal connection, making learning real both for the teacher and student.

You never know what the magic is until it's gone. We also take fire for granted—that is, until the ingredients are chopped but the stove won't light. Teaching a writing workshop by Zoom is like trying to cook a Chinese stir-fry in a microwave.

I set a deadline for committing to the resumed writing workshop. Two of the lagging Angsts rejoined. Another forgot the deadline but when reminded, said yes. Doubtful called me the night before the first workshop with a quiver of terror in her voice. She told me about her underlying medical conditions and her friend in Baton Rouge struggling to recover from the coronavirus. "I understand," I kept repeating, "whatever your decision is, I understand."

My own impatience overtook the charitable sympathy I should have been feeling as these writers struggled to face their fears of contagion by venturing out among others after months of lockdown. Once again, as with the grocery store security guard with her hand sanitizer protocols, the pandemic was bringing out the imp of the perverse in me, a brazen impetuosity that seldom surfaces. Fearless as I'd always been, blindly dashing about the globe through tropical jungles and perilous dictatorships, I've often been forced to acknowledge that my own foolhardiness hasn't always been courage but rather denial, a shellacked lack of understanding for the reasonable doubts others might feel. Even now, those who live safely cocooned in the remote suburbs consider me mad to live among the criminal perils of downtown New Orleans.

Should the occasion ever arise in a hospital, I've signed a do not resuscitate order. I'm convinced that, although it may be a prerequisite, not dying isn't the same as living. *So for God's sake, let's get on with our lives or pull the plug*, insisted my imp of the perverse, stomping its stumpy legs in a childish tantrum. But if the illusion of security was what other people needed, well, there wasn't enough money in the world to pay me to play the cop.

I'd already explained to the members that I wouldn't police what people wore on their faces or at what distance they chose to stand and sit. I also emphasized that I wasn't a group therapist, and that the subject of the pandemic shouldn't be broached in workshop discussions. By all means say what you like to each other, I emphasized, but the group focus is strictly literature and writing. That was a smart move, according to a member who works at the Tulane University Faculty of Public Health and Tropical Medicine. "All people want to talk about now is the virus," she said, "about which they're completely ignorant."

We finally met last Wednesday evening at a spacious Uptown house bordering leafy Audubon Park. At first, as people straggled in, the encounter felt like prisoners just released from solitary confinement entering a cellblock exercise yard, blinking and wary. Then we poured glasses of wine and opened up, delighted to return to this part of our lives. As we spread out in the airy living room, the three Angsts in face masks arrived late and took up perches in the far corners. Finally Doubtful, with whom I'd spoken the previous evening, made her entrance to everyone's relief. Our hostess had decided not to seat us around her long dining room table, where in past sessions we'd gathered elbow to elbow, seminar-style. I'd actually brought along several tabs of Xanax in case anyone had a panic attack. If there's anything more contagious than a virus, it's anxiety. Those whom I'd christened as "Doubtful and the Three Angsts"— you know, that famous COVID punk rock band—never lowered their masks, not even to snack or drink, and I had to strain to understand the little they said.

The other four members were as garrulous as ever, including the sole male writer, the only one to have recovered from a bout with the coronavirus.

The short stories we discussed from an anthology of southern fiction couldn't have been timelier. In both Erskine Caldwell's "Kneel to the Rising Sun" and Richard Wright's "Big Boy Leaves Home," defiant Black men are pursued by armed gangs of White vigilantes in rural towns during chilling chase scenes. Both stories are set during the hungriest depths of the Depression, and comparisons to the present moment were difficult to avoid. Now urban police forces have assumed the roles of redneck vigilantes in chasing and murdering poor Black men. What surprised me was that the only Black member, sitting in a corner wearing a face mask, didn't have more to say, nor did an older White woman also wearing a mask, someone who had grown up in a small town in the Louisiana countryside. Perhaps both stories hit too close to home.

The manuscripts we considered drew more discussion, leading us back to any writer's true home: the guitar of the imagination. We enthused about new chapters from two ongoing novels, one centered on a rape in a New Orleans mafia family and the other from a science fiction thriller about an alien takeover of earth engineered by a global chain of sinister physical fitness clubs. A short story set in the eighties during the AIDS epidemic in New Orleans, part of a collection of interrelated stories steeped in dark humor, brought us briefly back to the present pandemic, and I wondered aloud if the definition of comedy as "tragedy plus time" might one day apply to the current epidemic.

The critiques weren't as lively and specific as usual, and often I felt as if I were lecturing, but sitting together, face-to-face, with eight other writers was reinvigorating, a lost tableau from a canceled life. Three of the hesitant members scooted away as soon as the workshop ended. As the rest of us took seats on the front porch overlooking the park, the Black member took off her face mask and miraculously popped alive, telling hilarious stories about living with her large, intergenerational family during lockdown.

After a hardscrabble life, it seems that her elderly mother had been lining up at drive-through food pantries, although the family didn't need the free grub. To avoid personal contact, relief workers packed the boxes of food in car trunks so that drivers never saw what they'd been given. On the day of the granddaughter's virtual graduation from college, the whole family gathered in front of their house to wave to an orchestrated parade of well-wishers who drove past, honking and waving signs. Just as the parade was passing, everyone standing outside began to gag on a nauseating stench from the grandmother's car in the driveway. Inside the trunk they discovered a forgotten raw chicken from the food pantry, left there to rot for two weeks. So the cheering parade-goers greeted the proud college graduate dressed in her cap and gown as she was hosing out the trunk of her grandmother's car, dousing it with Pine-Sol.

Finally life seemed complete. I'd just heard my first funny pandemic story. "Tragedy plus time," I kept repeating to myself on the way home.

And these days, time can't pass fast enough.

7

Even at my age, I've never felt like an old man, but rather like a young one who has been around for a really long time. And I do go back. Not only was I at the Summer of Love in 1967 but the previous summer hitchhiked from San Francisco back to New Orleans through the Mohave Desert. But today this septuagenarian flower child wakes up feeling like an invalid. I know that those with severe medical conditions are often forced to become shut-ins, but now wonder if otherwise healthy shut-ins eventually develop the symptoms of the chronically ill: depression, hypochondria, agoraphobia, fatigue, along with minor aches and pains that signal approaching doom. The Center for Disease Control, intent on reining in the coronavirus with their rigorous regulations, seems to be creating an older generation of invalids. I can spend hours on the computer Googling my array of symptoms, which seem to evaporate as soon as the screen fades.

The latest alarming figures from the stock market of pandemic paranoia are in. As usual, no distinctions are made between contagions in congregate settings such as nursing homes, prisons, meat-packing plants, farm-worker barracks, and homeless shelters, where the majority of infections take place, and the person-to-person spread within open communities. According to the *New Yorker*, approximately a third of the deaths in this country have occurred among the residents and staff of nursing homes, yet this distinction is never made in pandemic statistics, frightening the general population even more. Because of a surge in case statistics, Florida, Texas, Arizona, and California, which previously had reopened partially, are now entering renewed lockdowns. And in many other states, including Louisiana, plans to move into a Phase II reopening are on indefinite hold. Those from sixteen southern and western states are barred from setting foot in the Northeast, and all Americans are prohibited entry into the European Union. There go my plans to hightail it to recently reopened Spain.

This approach recalls the community quarantines during the bubonic plague outbreaks in Europe of the Middle Ages, when travelers had to present their health certificates to pass through the guarded gateposts of walled towns. Actually, these community quarantines seem reasonable, locking down specific places rather than individuals in order to develop localized herd immunities. Worldwide, if all passenger flights had been canceled in late February, perhaps we could have avoided not only the zigzagging spikes of infection but the worst ardors of self-isolation and a crashing economy.

This June, now that the enemy is already thriving inside the wide-open gates of most communities in this country, the media blame the current spike on the unfettered bacchanalias of that most unmemorable holiday, Memorial Day. Incessant video images are broadcast of crowded beaches and pools, young people dancing wildly in packed bars and nightclubs, and insouciant youngsters raising beer mugs at adjacent tables. I suppose it would be politically incorrect to show images of young people marching shoulder to shoulder during the recent month of daily protest demonstrations or of rioters shoving against each other in the arson-lit night.

The consensus is that the young have caused the spike in cases.

That is, young fun, not young social conscience.

Leave it to Americans to portray a morally indifferent virus in such judgmentally Puritanical terms. Public health officials were quick to point out that teeming crowds of drunken Carnival visitors infected New Orleans, but out of feminist solidarity would have hesitated to blame the enormous demonstration in Madrid in support of International Women's Day on March 8 for infecting that city, as everyone in Spain claims it did. These health officials have replaced that dour Puritan patriarch Cotton Mather in portraying a virus that punishes "sinners in the hands of an angry God."

Recently I've been avoiding the national news to focus on local and international perspectives, trying to view the situation both up close and as part of a global picture. The unrelenting national news updates on the horrifying suffering the virus can cause are punishing. It's as if we had to endure months of daily programming on the multiple ways that diabetes or Parkinson's can destroy a person's health. The latest is that the coronavirus can provoke blood clots that result in paralyzing strokes.

What's clear is that the medical establishment doesn't understand exactly what this virus is, how it mutates and is transmitted, and in which ways it can attack the body. The ongoing uncertainty recalls the first few years of the AIDS epidemic, when some metro passengers donned face masks to ride through the gay neighborhood in San Francisco. Evidently you can get coronavirus in packed bars but not at massive street protests for good causes. You can get it at Carnival parades but not at feminist rallies. It doesn't kill children, except when infected kids swell up with immunological inflammation. It's most dangerous for the elderly, except, that is, for people between eighteen and twenty-nine, the new demographic under attack.

Who can make any sense of this poppycock?

Now in terms of hospital admissions and positive test results, the young seem to be those targeted by the virus. I feel deep sympathy for them, not because they've contracted an illness from which the majority will quickly recover, but because the lockdown has robbed them of their youth. I can't imagine what it must feel like to be yanked out of school, separated from their peers, laid off from their low-paying service jobs or internships, and confined inside with their parents or roommates all day and night. Their connection to a world in which they've been establishing their lives has been broken, and their sole consolation is scrolling through cell phones or the internet. Not only learning, but life itself has become remote. They've missed their senior proms, graduation ceremonies, the rush of freedom stepping onto a college campus during freshmen year, exploratory trips abroad, friends' weddings and engagement parties, and family members' funerals and burials. In short, they're been left bereft of the essential rituals with which we older adults initiated our lives and formed our social identities. It's no wonder that this past year forty-five thousand people have committed suicide, most of them teenagers or in their twenties.

And now, after one or two nights whooping it up in crowded bars, college students are publicly shamed. Some do, of course, get sick. Compared to their boomer parents, this generation may not be a particularly adventurous one to begin with, but this should maim them for life.

What young person wants to stay home and play it safe? From now on, this generation might.

As I approach my seventy-third birthday, I feel as if I've aged more in the past four months than in the last four years. I may be healthy, but am starting to feel like an invalid. Last night I dreamed that I was a tourist renting a hotel room in the French Quarter, which in itself suggests the onset of dementia, considering my animosity toward tourists. I was with two dowdy women tourists, and together we finally found an open hotel. My single room had a balcony, but I wondered what in the world I was doing there. Slowly the room filled with people milling about, introducing themselves, then wine corks popped, Styrofoam containers of food appeared, music was blaring, and my room was like—how can I describe it?—one of those wild bar scenes broadcast on the news in which the young are infected with the coronavirus. I slipped out of the party and walked into the hotel carriageway toward a wrought-iron gate that faced the street. I couldn't bring my hand to open it, much as I longed to step onto the sidewalk. I froze reaching for the gate handle, but just couldn't do it.

When I returned to my room, everyone was gone.

Then I lay down on the hotel bed. Of course, I woke from this dream in my own bed feeling claustrophobic, dreading the day and night ahead. The party was over and I was an invalid, or at least feeling like a young man who might have been around for far too long.

8

I feel fine. Yet according to the Center for Disease Control, feeling fine is now an alarming symptom.

Of a super-spreader.

Today, when I finally relent and go to have my hair cut in the French Quarter, I'm handed a two-page "COVID-19 Symptom Checker" questionnaire. A printout from a spectrum.health.org website, I don't know quite what to do with it, but it seems that giving it to me is required by law. I don't have any of the twelve symptoms mentioned, but when I return home the TV news informs me that my apparent health is a dangerous illusion. In a futile attempt to convince people not to gather tomorrow to celebrate July Fourth, we're told that many asymptomatic people are spreading the coronavirus, dangerous fools like me who "feel fine."

This advice leaves us no guard rails to clutch during a descent into mass hysteria.

According to Paul Romer, a Nobel Prize-winning economist, if the country continues this "seesaw pattern" of closing and reopening businesses in response to the latest pandemic statistics, the economy won't fully recover until 2028. He finds much of what the CDC reports as "bizarrely unhelpful," such as the advice today that asymptomatic people who feel fine may be the very super-spreaders we should most fear.

This is my first trip downtown during almost four months, and I'm one of only three other passengers on the "Walmart to Cemeteries" bus that takes me along Esplanade Avenue to the French Quarter, one that now passes every hour instead of every half-hour, as it used to. My Creole family lived in the Quarter from 1852 until the 1920s, establishing a tobacco shop on the corner of Chartres and St. Louis Streets, and I've always felt right at home the moment I step into my ancestral neighborhood. But now, walking the streets where I lived for twenty years, finally driven out by unrelenting vampire tours and the onslaught of mass tourism, I'm shocked by how desperate and abandoned the place feels, much more so than during the aftermath of Hurricane Katrina. In the wreckage after that disaster, the streets were seething with collective hope and defiance, but now are death-bed depressing. It's as if I'm in that episode of *The Twilight Zone* in which the lone survivor of an annihilating apocalypse roams through the ghost town of his old home.

Several of the smaller bars and restaurants have reopened, but I spot nobody inside. Both the bar and restaurant of the famous Arnaud's are boarded up with plywood. On the eve of the Fourth of July, only a few people stroll down Bourbon Street clutching cocktails in go-cups, pretending to have a blast on Desolation Row. I pass the occasional cluster of roly-poly tourists, some wearing face masks, waddling along as they stare at their phone screens, probably lost. Art galleries, museums, and most other cultural destinations remain closed. A six-seater fringed golf cart blaring music stops in front of a bar, where the drunken passengers jump out to gyrate on the sidewalk in a vulgar display that only emphasizes how forlorn the streets feel.

I'm relieved to be here with a practical mission: a long-needed haircut. Otherwise, this is neither charming nor fun.

The hairdresser's door is locked, so I put on my face mask and tap at the windowpane. The closed door is only one of the many regulations that the shop has to follow to meet city health standards. Inside are two hairdressers and only one other client, a shrunken elderly lady of some local renown, the originator of the green hand grenade cocktail, whose frizzed mop of dyed hair I first mistake for a Pomeranian lapdog perched on a towel. Mickey, the owner who cuts my hair, spritzes my fingers with gooey hand sanitizer. He's an expansive Cajun, usually jovial and loquacious, but I can tell something is wrong. He seems stressed out and fed up and, from what I can understand from the remarks he mumbles under his face mask, is worried to death about keeping his business open.

He has a long list of health department procedures to follow, special disinfectants in which he has to clean his tools, and mounting bills to pay, including overdue rent for the months the shop was closed. Although almost twenty thousand people lived here when I first moved home in 1996, over the past few years the neighborhood's permanent population has dwindled to 850 full-time residents, the size of a small country town. With no drop-by tourists and without even those flush weekend condo owners who occupy most of the Quarter's apartments, now sitting empty, who are his steady customers?

Another client arrives, a slovenly man who owns a fancy men's clothing shop on Royal Street, along with a few other commercial properties in the Quarter. Under his face mask, he's ranting that if Congress doesn't extend the federal unemployment benefits about to expire, "there'll be a revolution in this country. Hear what I'm saying, a revolution!" It seems odd that the proprietor of a shop that sells designer men's suits would be calling for a revolution, but evidently he can't pay his charming salesclerk's salary. After all, how many people in this sparsely populated, desperate neighborhood are looking for an Italian dress suit? He'd wanted to convert the space into a franchise ice cream shop, in which he could, as he puts it, "hire some monkey at eight bucks an hour to scoop ice cream," but the strict Vieux Carré Commission turned down any franchise applications for this historic neighborhood.

He and Mickey nod, shouting under face masks, agreeing about their dismal business futures, both regretful they've tried to reopen rather than closing for good. On paying, I feel guilty asking for the twenty dollar discount the shop has offered its regular customers to lure them back, but, frankly, that is partially why I'm here. As a writer and self-employed writing teacher, what are my own economic prospects?

I also have bills to pay, ones that won't wait until "the full economic recovery" predicted for 2028.

On my way to Canal Street, I skirt around that monument to tourist greed and corrupt city mismanagement, the ruins of the sixteen-story Hard Rock Hotel that collapsed during its shoddy construction last October. Located in the heart of downtown at the intersection of Canal and Rampart streets, the bodies of two workers are still rotting inside the rubble. During the past ten months little had been done to remove the towering disaster. To the horror of preservationists, two adjoining historic buildings were leveled to make way for the hotel's eventual demolition. After walking through the French Quarter, its streets emptied of the very tourist hordes this monolithic hotel was meant to house, my heart sinks even further as I gaze up at this chaotic emblem of commercial overexpansion and civic mismanagement.

Like the mishandling of the pandemic, this war-zone eyesore represents failure on so many levels, mostly of the imagination.

I'm the lone passenger on the sleek red Canal streetcar to City Park, a longer ride but one that runs every twenty minutes. The driver tells me that she often makes the trip with no passengers at all. At the end of the line, nobody is waiting to board. Frankly, I'm relieved to be back in the Faubourg St. John, that "false town" (from the French *faux*, meaning fake, and *bourg*, small town) on the outskirts of the once teeming, cosmopolitan French Quarter. Compared to my eerie trek through the city's center, it's comforting to be back in this gracious if bourgeois neighborhood filled with permanent residents walking their dogs, jogging, bicycling, pushing baby buggies, or ambling home from the grocery under rows of live oaks.

Here history remains intact. After all, without the people who belong to a place, history is just a pile of rotting lumber and crumbling bricks.

9

In August of 2006, while New Orleans was still reeling from Hurricane Katrina, I needed a break. So I decided to spend the month at a friend's vacant house in Pátzcuaro, Mexico. Compared to the daily chaos in New Orleans, Mexico felt like Switzerland: restaurants were open and clean, buses ran on schedule, ATMs worked, and the people seemed focused and industrious. Needless to say, few visitors ever compare Mexico to Switzerland, and frankly the country had never struck me in quite the same way during previous stays, but that impression was a measure of how topsy-turvy New Orleans felt at the time.

The evening before I caught my 5:30 a.m. flight home to New Orleans from the airport in Morelia, an hour's drive to the north, a Mexican friend introduced me to a local taxi driver who promised to pick me up at 3:30 in the morning. While packing, I wondered if I'd gone crazy to trust the word of a taxi driver I'd met in the public market to catch a flight that, if missed, would strand me in Michoacán for God knew how long. After all, the Mexican *mañana* is similar to the New Orleans term "real soon," although slightly more urgent and reliable.

Yet the taxi driver was beeping his horn in front of my door ten minutes early.

Fast-forward fourteen years to pandemic New Orleans: yesterday I had an emergency dental appointment Uptown for 3:45 p.m. A week before, a reconstructed front tooth had fallen out when I tore into an extra-crispy fried chicken wing after a writing workshop, so I socially distanced my alarming jack-o-lantern smile at home all weekend. When stepping out, I gratefully wore the required face mask everywhere, appreciating it for the first time for the way it hid any dental flaws. I called the trusty United Cab Company, on which I had relied for years, for a cab to pick me up at 2:45. Always punctual and efficient, I should have known something wasn't working when the hold time was twenty minutes. The dispatcher mumbled something about "this situation." I emphasized the purpose of my ride: "urgent medical appointment."

When the cab still hadn't arrived by 3:20, a neighbor offered to drop everything, gave me a ride, and I arrived at the dentist's on time. On the way back, I wasn't about to be stood up by another taxi, so I took a meandering two-hour route on streetcar lines. But once home I wasn't wearing a newly minted smile when I received a landline message from the taxi driver, clocked at 3:40, informing me that he was downstairs waiting, almost an hour late.

I called United to complain. The dispatcher apologized, claiming that the company was, as he put it, "a mess": few drivers were on the job, many working cabbies didn't show up, picked up passengers late, and complained they weren't showing any profit. Obviously our small local population, few of whom were going anywhere, couldn't support a fleet of efficient taxis. I tried to sympathize through the clenched teeth of my bright new smile.

While in the shower that evening at 9:30, I received another voice message. This one was from my doctor, who wanted to discuss a non-virus test result. I'd been trying to reach him at his clinic for days. Evidently now he could talk to me, at almost ten at night.

I was having a Katrina moment. And no, this time I didn't long to escape to Mexico, no longer anything like Geneva. At least there the drug cartels are playing Robin Hood by distributing free food in their starving neighborhoods.

So pity this cranky old White man, one who sounds like a privileged brat, complaining about unreliable taxis and overworked doctors. I hear sirens shrieking through the night, either from an ambulance delivering a coronavirus patient to the hospital or a police cruiser responding to a shooting. We're in a crisis moment, when the basic services we once took for granted are overstretched to the breaking point. We can't rely on anything working right. When I finally do reach a company representative to resolve any problem, it's invariably a stressed out younger woman "working from home" with a baby crying or a dog barking in the background.

I don't need to socially distance. I've given up and won't try to do anything once considered normal unless it's an emergency. When I'd returned home this evening, an ominous murder of carrion crows was circling the sky. Their shrill caws echoed inside the foyer of the Luling Mansion, where walking through the deserted purple and scarlet chambers on the second floor and climbing the stairs toward the mute ebony clock on the landing, I wondered what kind of sign that was.

10

Never in my wildest imagination would it have occurred to me that precisely now, at the height of a global pandemic, the film crew would return here to finally shoot the Amazon Prime vampire movie, *Black as Night.*

The original four-day schedule proposed for the middle of March, when the crew painted the second-story walls in the plague color palette, has now ballooned into a two-week ordeal because of the sanitization requirements imposed by state and city health departments, along with the production company's demanding insurance company. Try to picture a crowded, chaotic film shoot combined with a hospital ward in a decaying 150-year-old building that hasn't even been cleaned—much less sanitized—in decades. Visqueen screens will be hung from the eighteen-foot ceilings to separate the crew and actors from us four tenants. Hard to summarize, the following email from the location manager intends more to placate the insurance company rather than to assure residents in outlining these punctilious precautions. The document reads much like the endless pages of preventive bubonic plague edicts in Daniel Defoe's novel:

- All Cast and Crew will be COVID tested from 1 to 5 times/ week
- All locations will be sanitized prior to entry and after leaving the location
- Hand-washing Stations will be placed on and around set
- Social Distancing will be enforced by a COVID Health Manager and/or Health Supervisor
- Hospital Grade Hand Sanitizer will be available
- All crew members will don PPE Gear (N95 Masks, Goggles, Face Shields, etc.)

If you would like to remain in your apartments during prep and wrap, we will provide full PPE (Personal Protective Equipment: N95 masks, goggles and Face Shields) to all tenants in the building for entering and exiting your apartment. The Prep and Wrap teams will also be in full gear.

- Prep and Wrap teams will be putting up visqueen to separate you from the rooms where we will be working, in the case that you need to come and go.
- The building will be sanitized prior to entry and after leaving each day. I am happy to have a meeting with all of you (social distancing or Zoom) with our Sanitizing Specialist on the show. She can explain all levels and products that will be utilized.
- No one will enter ANY of your apartments during this shoot.

All of this, as exacting as it sounds, is supposed to take place in the middle of hurricane season, when the daily outside heat index reaches a scorching 105–110 degrees. Only a single rusty window AC unit wheezes on the cavernous second floor, where there are no bathrooms and only one working electrical outlet. Rather than bikinis and towels in this steam bath, the crew will be covered in suffocating hospital-grade plastic PPE, including masks and face shields. The cast will at least be performing under cover of darkness, from dusk to dawn, as you might expect in a production with such a clunky title as *Black as Night*. It is to be one in a series of Amazon Prime Videos called "Welcome to the Blumhouse," described as "eight terrifying genre movies," preceded by *The Lie* (2018), *Nocturne* (2020), and *Black Box* (2020).

Yvette is the shoot location manager, a stressed out woman with a piquant sense of humor who lives in the neighborhood. She tells me that becoming a film crew member on this production is akin to taking convent Holy Orders. Everyone working on the movie must remain masked at all times on the sweltering set, as well as be tested for coronavirus every other day, at a clinic downtown used by the players in the National Football League. If one person should test positive, the production will be halted while the entire crew quarantines for two weeks. Crew members must enter the grounds through one gate and leave through another, where their body temperatures will be monitored. Yvette emphasizes that this is the first production that the state has authorized to proceed since the filming shutdown at the beginning of the pandemic in March and so is projected to be something of a trial run for future shoots in Louisiana. For insurance purposes, they must rigorously follow every guideline.

Which means that we tenants will be relocated to the downtown Hilton for ten days.

"Wait a minute," I protest. Once again, the pandemic brings out the red-faced imp of the perverse in me, furious that I'm being forced into an irrational activity for what some oblivious bureaucrat considers my own good. "Isn't that where they put the homeless people this April during the beginning of the pandemic? I refuse to stay at any hotel. Their corridors, elevators, and air filtration systems are incubators of infection. Especially one where the homeless camped out for the past couple of months. And the restaurants downtown are all closed. Where will I eat?"

After a long negotiation on my part, it's agreed that the tenant relocation won't last the originally proposed ten days but only during the three days of the actual film shoot, and we'll be reimbursed with a hotel stipend no matter where else we may chose to go, plus a per diem.

I still refuse to budge. "I'm writing a book, and all my notes, books, and papers are here in my office."

I picture myself as the Bernie Sanders of the Luling Mansion, labor standing up to management. After living for twenty years in the French Quarter, I'm used to bartering with film companies. They need neighbors' cooperation more than we need their star-studded intrusions into our lives. While living on Dumaine Street, the production company of *Twelve Years a Slave* paid me a thousand dollars to locate a camera on my balcony adjacent to Madame John's Legacy, a historic landmark in which three minutes of the film was shot.

After further talks, it's agreed that I can stay if I commit to self-quarantine in my third-floor apartment for the three days of the film shoot, not sticking my nose outdoors for any reason.

And speaking of my nose, first I must be tested. They will drive me to the National Football League testing site. "No," I counter, digging in my heels. "I don't want to share a car with a stranger to go to some football clinic. Unsafe at any speed."

Finally they agree to send someone to test me at home.

I resist. Rumpelstiltskin throws another tantrum. Even though I'm asymptomatic and "feeling fine," now viewed as the red flag of a super-spreader, what if some unreliable test says I'm positive? That would further cancel my life, blowing it to smithereens. Especially if I'm not.

I counter that I'd have to be tested at home every other day for a week.

Nothing doing, the film company says.

Later, Yvette confides in me that mine was a wise decision. Several crew members tested positive one day, negative the next. Everyone on the purple and scarlet vampire movie set has the plague-testing jitters, awaiting their latest results from one day to the next. Their livelihoods, along with the film production schedule, depend on having a cotton swab jabbed up their noses. Yvette swears she wouldn't submit to this kind of personal hell unless they were paying her well, which, of course, they are. After four months out of work, she really needs the job.

The crew constructs a faux cemetery of conventional tombstone markers in an empty lot across the street, adjacent to St. Louis Cemetery Number Three, in which my family is buried. I suppose that the archdiocese in charge of St. Louis wouldn't permit vampires to go gallivanting all night between the above ground tombs of the city's ancestors, primarily those from old Creole families. As the pandemic numbers begin to spike again after July Fourth, I stand on my balcony shuddering at the creepiness of this Potemkin village of the undead across the street.

Then, for three days and nights during the last week of August, I remain isolated in my apartment, adjusting curtains and shutters to block out the blinding klieg lights aimed at my floor-to-ceiling windows, which cast my rooms in the eerie glow of an alien invasion. A crew member leaves my mail at my front door and takes down my garbage. I usually tend to keep vampire hours—observing what the French call *la nuit blanche*, or going to bed just before dawn—but don't hear a peep, whimper, or howl from the cast members one floor below.

Or should I say, from the vampires of color downstairs. *Black as Night*, as I learn later, isn't just a racist cliché, but a thematic title. I'm told that this is part of the "Welcome to the Blumhouse" Amazon series is geared for teeny-boppers and features Black vampires.

During the worst era of racial unrest in this country since the late sixties, with its daily Black Lives Matter protests, and amid the medical horrors of a seemingly unstoppable killer virus disproportionally taking the lives of Black Americans, I find myself living on the set of a Black vampire movie, imprisoned in my apartment. Evidently Black lives do matter, even among the undead. I listen to the shocking TV and radio news of daily protests, riots, and soaring coronavirus death rates on headphones, so that the blaring distress of the outside world won't be picked up by the sensitive set-microphones on the floor below, where Black actors impersonate vampires in ornate purple and scarlet chambers.

My quarantine among the bloodsuckers ends, I'm paid, the film shoot finally wraps up, and yet again I catch myself asking that fateful question pivotal to the crisis moment of every tragic plotline, "What else can go wrong?"

And as I bustle about with relief, arranging the plants on my balcony shifted to accommodate the vampire movie shoot, little do I suspect that the worst is yet to come.

11

When I finally emerge, I notice a piece of paper Scotch-taped to my front door.

An eviction notice.

This formal notice to vacate the premises by August 31 is dated July 24, the first day that evictions are again legal in Louisiana. It's signed by someone whom I'll call Callus Dikhedson, an ambulance-chasing personal injury lawyer who three months ago purchased this building.

I'm in shock. As the oldest tenant, one who has lived here for more than five years, I've survived the rocky transitions between three different owners and six property managers. The latest manager was named Delirio—I couldn't make this up—who quit after three months.

I'd moved in while a crew was filming a zombie apocalypse movie, and now I'd be leaving in the wake of a vampire film. How could I find a new apartment and pack up a lifetime of belongings, including the musty relics from four generations of a New Orleans family, in thirty days?

Who is this man who would evict a seventy-three-year-old in the middle of a global pandemic?

I'd only met this Dikhedson character twice, and his bluster reminded me of Donald Trump, another lord of all he surveys. He arrived at my door one afternoon to record the measurements of the apartment, supposedly for a blueprint he was drawing up of the building. While his meek, masked assistant scurried behind him, a young woman who I suspected was his mistress, he puffed out his chest to inform me that he was not only a lawyer but an engineer, among his many other accomplishments. On this, his only visit to my apartment, he seemed stunned by the view from my balcony of the tops of live oaks that framed the lit copula of Our Lady of the Holy Rosary across Esplanade Avenue and visibly impressed by the décor and antiques.

His eyes took immediate possession of my home.

"Did you know that the floor is asbestos tiling riddled with fissures," I asked the personal injury attorney who had made a killing on asbestos-exposure cases.

His face clouded. No, he didn't. "Well," he replied, "the tiles are encapsulated." That simply means painted.

"And cracking," I added, hoping to quench the greed in his eyes.

The second time I met him, while I was taking down the garbage in a ratty T-shirt and cargo shorts, he was charging past the mute ebony grandfather clock on the landing, up one of the twin curved staircases to the third floor. Cocktail in hand, he was wearing a shiny, white suit, followed by a retinue of equally natty corporate types. When I pretended to admire his white suit, he told me that he was dressed as a "plantation owner," now that he was one, or so thought this naïve midwesterner of Scandinavian descent. He was trying to throw a garden party during a rainstorm to impress his law partners and potential condo buyers with this, the vast manor of his feudal domain. Obviously converting this sparsely inhabited tenement of ten apartments into condos was his game plan, beginning with mine. As we later stood at the leaking, rusted front door watching the torrents of an afternoon thunderstorm soak the front lawn of his garden party, this Yankee dressed in a white plantation-owner suit struck me as pathetic as F. Scott Fitzgerald's Great Gatsby, basking in reflected glamour. His swaggering grandiosity was of the kind displayed only by the most ingenuous of men, those convinced that the world is their oyster even while wading through a fetid cesspool.

At the moment, I was wondering what would happen when the Great Gatsby met "The Fall of the House of Usher."

I say this because the gothic Luling Mansion is a reincarnation of Edgar Allan Poe's collapsing House of Usher. Its basic infrastructure hasn't been renovated since the twenty-two room Italian palazzo, constructed in 1865, was divided into ten rental apartments in 1934 by a new owner. A few years before I moved in it had been inherited by the Barthé family, the descendants of Earl Barthé, a celebrated plasterer who perfected the walls, ceilings, chandelier medallions, and the death masks above the crown moldings on the second floor. Attached to the mansion for sentimental reasons as the masterpiece of their patriarch's trade, these Creoles of color managed the property in a chaotic, laissez-faire manner, not sure what to do with the crumbling building and unable to afford its upkeep. Three years ago the Louisiana Trust for Historic Preservation listed it as among the "Nine Most Endangered Historic Buildings in New Orleans" and posted an alarming "demolition by neglect" notice on the front gate, citing "decay, visible water damage, and lack of basic maintenance." Two years ago, when Earl Barthé's daughter, Miss Terry, passed away from asbestos-related mesothelioma, her heir, a young niece from Atlanta, floundered. She put the mansion in the hands of yet another real estate agent, and when the looming white elephant made even Delirio so delirious that he quit, she decided to sell.

On the day I discover Dikhedson's notice to vacate, I send him an email stating that I have never missed a rent payment during my long tenancy and asking for at least two months to complete the move. I explain that "to find another apartment and move all of my many possessions in a single month during a global pandemic are together overwhelming. Not to mention just after my voluntary quarantine for the movie shoot. I have a serious heart condition, with two stents in my heart, and have undergone both a previous heart attack as well as open heart surgery. I don't think I could survive the stress of such a sudden move. I hope that we can negotiate this amicably, and avoid any long, drawn-out eviction proceedings. Please call me at your earliest convenience to discuss this situation."

Dikhedson's one word response: "No."

I immediately contact the Southeast Louisiana Legal Services, whose office, of course, is closed during the pandemic. Finally I'm put in touch with a pro bono housing lawyer working from home, a capable young woman named Hannah Adams, who specializes in the evictions of the poor, elderly, or disabled. She tells me that because of the coronavirus crisis, there's a parallel epidemic of evictions and that she spends every morning in eviction court. She writes to Dikhedson "to request that you give Mr. Nolan an extension until September 15 as a reasonable accommodation for his disability under the Fair Housing Act." She attaches a letter from my cardiologist, who describes my coronary artery disease and asks the landlord to "please afford your tenant every reasonable exemption in light of his elevated vulnerability to adverse clinical outcomes should he become ill with COVID-19."

For several weeks there's no response.

So from self-isolation I'm pitched into a whirl of real estate agents, public transportation, lawyers, movers, and packing supply stores, meanwhile dreading possible court appearances or an unexpected sheriff's eviction, during which the cops show up to throw your belongings on the street. While my landlord treats me as if I'm a conniving criminal, others consider me an invalid, yet I feel like neither. Actually, I don't have a moment to feel anything, but spin headlong into that tizzy of adrenaline-fueled mania called "moving." In the oppressive August heat I no longer sit on the balcony at sunset, communing with the spirit of the eternal live oak whose branches once seemed to cover and protect me.

I don't have time to think about the pandemic, to be afraid of contagion or become enraged about politics, to mourn or fret.

I swing into the high anxiety of fight-or-flight mode, simultaneously both fighting and fleeing. My scowling imp of the perverse, fretting about the frivolities of grocery hand sanitizer and student face masks, inflates into an embattled giant, wondering where he'll next cook, eat, sleep, and write. Scouting the French Quarter for rental signs, I pace the streets of my ancestral neighborhood in which I'd previously lived for twenty years before relocating to Faubourg St. John. Of course, none of the real estate agencies are actually open, so I waste a lot of time playing phonetag with agents' cell phones.

Half of the apartments in the ghost town of the Quarter are now either for sale as luxury condos or for rent. Prices are negotiable. I visit about a dozen apartments, most unsuitable as a future home. One doesn't have a closet, another no stove, only a hot plate. The majority have been recently renovated into snazzy, open spaces with granite-countertop kitchen islands, recessed lighting, and other contemporary design motifs alien to my taste in traditional architecture. These pricey little units are meant for young people with futons and Kindles, not an older writer with a towering mountain of boxes crammed with books and papers, a New Orleans native loaded down with his grandparents' armoires, cane-backed chairs, prie-dieu, and cedar chest.

Meanwhile I edit my life down to a portable size, throwing out clothes I'll never wear again, books I'll never read or hope to reread, exotic keepsakes from my travels to which I'd become attached over the years but no longer serve any earthly purpose. Even as the pile of taped boxes takes over the apartment, many of the decisions are heart-wrenching: do I really need two gumbo pots, both my grandmother's and my mother's? I guard with possessive affection my rough drafts of published and future books, correspondence with editors and far-flung writer friends, and stacks of collaged journals. An archivist at the New York Public Library expressed an interest earlier in the spring in acquiring my papers, but now the library is closed and the archivist in quarantine. Perhaps there's no future for this voluminous pile of stuff, but it represents the essence of who I'd once been and continue to be, so I keep most of it.

Finally around mid-August, Gary, an alert friend visiting from Alabama, spots a promising "For Rent" sign in the last block of Bourbon Street, the so-called Bend on Bourbon, where the street comes to a dead end at Pauger. It's a quiet, elegant block, despite the rowdy images conjured by the street name. The first-floor townhouse apartment is two doors down from Esplanade Avenue into the Marigny neighborhood. Go-getter Gary looks up the photos online and is so pleased by what he sees—814 square feet of recently refinished hardwood floors, spacious high ceilings, chandeliers with plaster medallions, marble mantelpieces, sliding pocket doors, and a courtyard—that he bypasses playing phonetag with the agent's cell and texts him in my name, since I don't text. I immediately get an appointment for an agent's viewing.

One look and I decide, yes, this will be fine. I was searching for magic, but you can't summon magic. It has to find you. The landlord, Mr. Persons, happens to be a cousin of Truman Persons, the New Orleans-born writer whose last name was later changed to Capote.

The real estate rigmarole—the online application that Gary helps me to fill out, gathering the banking information for a credit check, meeting with the landlord, a visit to the desert island of my bank to secure the cashier's check for the first month's rent and deposit, which I have to deliver to an empty real estate office then later pay yet another visit to this catacomb to sign the lease—is almost more than I can take at the moment. This is a process stressful enough during normal times, but during the pandemic lockdown when nobody and nothing are working as they should, often feels insurmountable. It seems as if I'm trying to launch a business after a nuclear apocalypse has wiped out most of the earth's population.

But with my friends' support, I do it.

I now have a new place in which to move, if only I can deal with the timing demands of the Great Gatsby, the unreliability of moving companies during the epidemic, and the four flights of steps that lead up to my third-story apartment. Trudging up and down the outside granite staircase during the blast furnace of summer heat is like scaling the Pyramid of the Sun at the ruins of Chichén-Itzá in the Yucatan.

Not to mention the constant hurricanes threatening the city, at one point two in the same week. A direct hit on the city could bring any moving plans to an abrupt halt. I'm glued to weather advisories, in which New Orleans often features prominently in the "Cone of Uncertainty" along the Gulf Coast.

Moving in here five years ago, while sweating friends helped me to lug my more fragile possessions up the endless staircases, I often paused to announce, "Next stop, assisted living." Never in my wildest dreams did I imagine that my next stop would be Bourbon Street during a plague year.

12

Much like during the wildest escapades of my youth, I don't know what I'm doing, but I'm doing it full speed ahead. One mover, an amiable Creole of color who seems to know a lot about transporting armoires and other antiques, drives his crew past the house after he visits me to offer an appraisal. Yet once his middle-aged movers have gotten an eyeful of the vertiginous staircases of the gloomy mansion, his cell phone ignores my increasingly frantic calls. I finally locate a mover with an open office, in which the landline is answered by the owner from 8:00 a.m. to 5:00 p.m. seven days a week—a comforting luxury during this pandemic lockdown—and we agree on a time and date. The Great Gatsby has backed off from his pressing deadlines. The bullying lawyer Dikhedson is obviously cowered by my own attorney's invocation of the Americans with Disabilities Act.

What remains to be seen is how I will pay for this move. And on September 10, the emblematic peak date of hurricane season, the answer arrives fifteen minutes before the movers do, while I'm taking a last glance at my email before zipping up the laptop in its carrying case. I can hardly believe the timing. I've been awarded a United States Artists' Relief Grant of $5,000, which will be deposited into my checking account days after I provide my banking information. At the urging of a friend, two weeks ago I'd applied for assistance to the national arts agency headquartered in Chicago, mentioning my twelve published books, the canceled writing workshops, and the word that undoubtedly riveted the agency's attention to my immediate need: *eviction*. I dash off a quick message of gratitude to the Artist Relief Manager, Lee Heinemann, commenting on the uncanny timing of the news. And he immediately responds: "the best with your move."

Ten minutes later, four fit, young Black men arrive at the appointed time, none wearing masks. I resist the temptation to mention the Black vampires who have recently vacated the now empty movie set on the second floor, but spookiness is also a communicable disease. Fist bumps suffice, but I don't want to pretend I'm pals with them. I haven't slept and am delirious. I point at this piece of furniture and then that, all of which somehow disappear down four flights of stairs. I pray. A St. Jude candle smolders on the empty marble mantelpiece.

One mover bales out halfway through the morning. He can't take the heat and the steps. The crew captain calls in another, who never arrives. "O St. Jude, Apostle and Martyr," I pray. "It's me again, that nutty writer from St. Dominic's in San Francisco. Remember my AIDS tests? Help me in my present and urgent petition. . . ."

Somehow it happens, as moves tend to do. Several pieces of furniture arrive broken—the rickety armoire and cedar chest. Now the turntable won't spin and the mantle clock won't tick. Other priceless items are lost, like my grandfather's gold jewelry and my passport. In my hectic packing during the sudden move, I realize that perhaps I was trying to erase myself. In that woozy state between dying and not dying is a subconscious instinct toward self-erasure, a letting go of the self. I was and still am, but as García Lorca writes, "*Ya no soy yo/ ni mi casa es ya mi casa.*" (Now I'm no longer myself / and this house isn't my home.)

I leave only one thing at the Luling Mansion, a small oil painting of the many-armed Kali, Hindu goddess of death, destruction, and renewal. This is a particularly menacing portrait of the gruesome deity dressed in solid black, her six arms clutching knives, hatchets, and skulls. As a parting gesture on the day I move, I roll it up tightly to tuck behind the monumental gilded mirror hanging over the marble mantle in my bedroom, its reflection beclouded by 150 years, as a hex on the Great Gatsby, who is evicting me. And I confess to a shameful rush of schadenfreude when I learn, months later, that Callus Dikhedson and his third wife, with whom he'd recently reconciled, along with their whole family, came down with severe cases of the coronavirus. And that he was soon informed by the Louisiana Landmarks Society that if he converted the rental apartments into luxury condos, as planned, he'd lose the building's historic-status tax exemptions, canceling any projected profit. Except for two occupied apartments, the gothic mansion now sits almost empty in gloomy abandon, and I hear that the swaggering "plantation owner" is seldom seen on the premises, over which Kali continues to cast her spell from behind the opaque mantle mirror.

I spend the next month on Bourbon Street with a box cutter in hand, shelving books and stacking crates of files. Donald Trump is still the president, the coronavirus is spiking again, and the election furor heating up, not that I pay much attention to what's happening around me. I'm squatting on these shiny hardwood floors, sorting through art, trying to make this house my home, to piece together whoever I still may be from whatever is left of who I once was.

I miss the view from my balcony at the Luling Mansion and my ancient live oak, but not much else. Soon after I move in a huge belladonna tree in the courtyard bursts into bloom, bathing my evenings with white trumpet flowers of somnambulant fragrance.

13

It's mid-November and, the last box unpacked, I emerge as if from a cave into the glare of a national drama with a plot as ancient as a Sophocles play. A mad dethroned king refuses to leave the palace while a plague rages throughout the populace. His usurper is an older nobleman who was a courtier to the previous king. This wise, fatherly figure has claimed the throne and promises to restore unity and healing in the pestilence-ravaged kingdom, now savagely divided between allegiances to the competing monarchs. Two month's before the coronation, the delusional king wanders the emptying chambers of his scandal-embroiled palace, ignoring the plague and fulminating like Lear with bitter accusations in a maelstrom of his own making: "Blow, winds, and crack your cheeks. Rage, blow, / You cataracts and hurricanes . . . / And thou, all-shaking thunder, / Strike flat the thick rotundity o' th' world . . . / That makes ungrateful man."

I wish this tragedy had a more resounding title, something Shakespearean, perhaps in Greek or Latin, other than the risible name of a reality TV personality: "Donald Trump." But then again, leave it to America to star Daffy Duck in its remake of a classic blood drama.

Cocooned for two months in the self-preoccupations of my move, I'm shocked by the rapidly deteriorating world around me. Coronavirus infections have spiked to a level far surpassing the initial outbreak in March. Most of Europe and much of this country are once again entering full lockdowns. Breadlines of the unemployed waiting in cars stretch for miles along highways as the economy continues to tank. The election is over for everyone but delusional King Trump, who tweets a paranoid vitriol of false accusations that has everyone shaking their heads in dismay except for his enraged followers, who unfortunately comprise 49 percent of the population. In any other country, or at any other moment in history, this would feel like the prelude to a civil war. Yet now people aren't allowed to gather publicly to further inflame each other, and most are trying hard to survive hunger, isolation, and infection.

Let the deposed monarch tweet on.

Evidently, during August, while I was obsessively stacking pyramids of boxes and scrambling to contact real estate agents, the suddenly unconfined Germans and British were flocking to the beaches of Spain for their traditional summer vacations. The sangria flowed, and so did the virus. Now all three countries are once again in strict lockdowns, along with most of their neighbors, particularly France. Europeans are self-disciplined enough to give up almost anything except for their sacrosanct *vacances en août*.

We Americans living along the Gulf Coast aren't so fond of August, a month approaching the peak date of the hurricane season: September 10. We have too many traumatic memories of floods, evacuations, and utter devastation. Luckily, I was spared a storm on that ill-chosen day of my move, but during this season thirty named hurricanes threatened the United States, five of which hit Louisiana. On October 28 only Hurricane Zeta actually passed through New Orleans, where, along with street-flooding and toppled trees, 60 percent of the city lost power, many for up to a week. Here at the Bend on Bourbon Street, the lights went out for the seven lantern-lit hours on a balmy fall night, and a single flowerpot toppled over in the courtyard. Born during a hurricane, I hate to admit how much I love these storms, exulting in my own survival while an enraged sky swirls around me.

The hurricane hit the city a week before the presidential election, a storm of a far more disturbing nature. For weeks after, mail-in and absentee ballots are being counted and recounted. A wide splotch of blood red remains at the center of the country as an ever-expanding rim of cool blue takes over the coastal states. The Democratic Party's fearmongering of coronavirus infections at crowded polling places on November 3 is partially responsible for the crates of paper ballots overflowing the fluorescent-lit hangars of overworked election officials, giving rise to Trump's unsubstantiated accusations of voter fraud.

On November 3, I walk three blocks to vote at the Marigny fire station. The voting booth is in the empty, open-air garage in which the fire engine is usually parked, I'm one of only three voters at the site, and the whole process takes two minutes. How much easier it would have been to set up similar neighborhood sites in schools and churches across the country, broadcast the results electronically on election night, and thus avoid this prolonged avalanche of paper verification. No coronavirus infections at polling places on election day have been reported, even as Trump continues to demand the repetitive recount of the mail-in and drop-box ballots that he claims hijacked the election.

To my mind, the fear of on-site polling infection is yet another example of the overreach of public health policies that have further divided the country, ending in chaos. I'm not quite sure what the Democratic Party had in mind: to guarantee voter participation, to kick-start a preemptive Biden victory, or out of a genuine concern about possible infections on the day of the election. The endless lines of voters snaking outside of polling places at early voting sites seem to belie any concerns about mass infections. What difference would it have made if people amassed in close contact on the day of the election itself, or a week before? This early voting push has only resulted in Trump's delirious invectives about fraud and put the normally smooth rituals of a democratic election on precarious grounds.

Advising caution should be commended, but sowing needless fear can only result in the erosion of public trust, both in electoral institutions and public health policies. Consequently, this Thanksgiving nobody seems to believe the sound warnings about avoiding the airports usually packed during this traditional holiday of family reunions. Million of people are catching flights to feast with relatives, for exactly the same reason that the Chinese traveled widely during their two-week lunar New Year holiday in February at the beginning of the epidemic, when the virus transmission first exploded. Now we're awaiting the second—or is it the third?—surge in coronavirus hospitalizations from the travelers who passed through those incubators of infection. Americans can no more resist their Thanksgiving flights home than the Chinese can forgo New Year's travel or the Germans and Brits can skip their August vacations in Spain. These dates are hard-wired into the holiday calendars of our cultures.

A lot of suffering could be spared, and the unrelenting advice silenced, if worldwide public health authorities simply canceled all passenger flights for the time being. It would send the further spread of the virus to a screeching halt and simplify the byzantine restrictions of who can fly where, which borders are open to whom, and the bureaucracy of travel health documents and arrival quarantines. Italy, the Western country that suffered the most at the outbreak of the virus, now has it right: nobody can travel more than fifty kilometers anywhere within the country. In Madrid, certain hard-hit neighborhoods are off-limits to those who live in other parts of the city. I find myself screaming at the worsening pandemic news on TV: *lockdown communities, stupid, not individuals.* This was the way that the bubonic plague was eventually defeated in Europe.

The much-touted herd immunity that the new vaccines are supposed to build could be achieved if everyone just stayed put. Not locked indoors, alone or with their families, but just going about their normal lives in the place where they belong.

14

There's an old blues song about meeting the devil at the crossroads and trading your soul for what he promises. And what the devil at the crossroads offers now isn't musical genius but literally the whole world, or at least a fast and easy access to it. Yet the devil knows what he's doing. This is where pandemics are born and thrive: at the crossroads along borders.

A deeply entrenched globalism is now taken for granted. We've claimed the right to live everywhere simultaneously, and this will continue to spawn worldwide epidemics well into the twenty-first century. As a world traveler, I'm guiltier of this than most. I understand the itch for the open road, those explorations that air travel now makes so easy. Why lead only one life when, boarding pass in hand, you can live so many?

Resisting outside infections is one reason that we mammals instinctively gather in protective herds. We're so unlike those insects with hard-shelled carapaces, the ants and bees that live and die as one in the massive collectives of their hives. Single ants and bees don't crawl off to die alone. When these insects are infected or poisoned, the whole hive dies. Their existence and fates are as interconnected and global as ours have become, but as hive creatures, they're much less susceptible.

Yet for us, leaving the herd can be fatal. The history of mass human migrations is a tragic one of pandemics and extinctions. Almost all of us who live in the American hemispheres are here today only because early European colonists and conquistadores killed off 90 percent of the Indigenous populations with massive contagions of their foreign diseases: measles, smallpox, bubonic plague, influenza, cholera, chicken pox, scarlet fever, and yellow fever. From the New World, the colonists brought home with them not only gold and tuberculosis but a deadly strain of syphilis, one previously unknown in Europe. And this is just a single example in a long history of how human displacement from one herd to another has inevitably ended in epidemic disease and massive mortalities.

Of course, this was long before the global hives of airports that now connect us. In the meantime, science has made many advances with antibiotics and vaccines, but human immunology hasn't changed much since 1492. When Columbus first set foot in Hispaniola, 250,000 Indigenous peoples were living on the island, presently divided into Haiti and the Dominican Republic. Without firing a shot, only 14,000 of these native peoples remained in 1517. At the moment I'm sitting in New Orleans, adjacent to our Caribbean cousin Haiti, with which we share so much history because of the European viruses that killed off most of those native to these Louisiana swamps.

This week a new, much more infectious strain of the coronavirus has developed in England, and fifty countries have prohibited air travel to and from the United Kingdom. Like neighboring France, some countries even have halted land, rail, and maritime travel in and out of this viral hot spot. The prime minister has canceled Christmas celebrations, both public and private, only two weeks before the disastrous consequences of the final deadline of the Brexit policy further isolate now not-so-merry old England from the rest of the world.

And we wonder why so many virulent forms of populist nationalism, such as Trump's and Boris Johnson's, have come raging back within this international global village created during the past half century. Make America great again. Britain for the Brits. Build that wall and get these foreign germs out of here. This pandemic—what Trump calls the Kung Flu—has become a political metaphor. Our corruption comes from outside—from *them*.

All viruses mutate, and I've been wondering when the coronavirus would. The crowning irony is that these variants are appearing not only in England but in South Africa and Brazil, just as the first vials of vaccines are being distributed worldwide, almost as if the virus were anticipating our next move in some diabolical chess game. Viruses aren't static. One theory is that in 1494, a milder form of syphilis, then known as yaws or lepra, already existed in Europe before the first colonists returned to Naples from the New World. But the more virulent strain brought from the Americas eventually caused this domesticated virus to mutate into the lethal disease that syphilis became during the next five centuries.

With air travel, the viral variants that once took centuries to develop can now happen within months. But if the extensive global air grid we've created continues to exist and we are to survive as a species, it needs emergency shut-off valves, like gas lines during a forest fire. And we travelers need to accept, for perhaps extended periods, being stuck where we live to cohabit with our neighbors' down-home germs, which threaten us much less severely than those from halfway around the world, as served up in the simmering viral Crock-Pots of airport departure lounges.

Yet I'm no hypocrite. I'm thinking this as an inveterate globetrotter, a former expatriate, someone who has never been content unless packing a suitcase to escape from the tedium of being where I am at the moment. For years I lived between Barcelona and San Francisco, and then between New Orleans, San Francisco, and Madrid. Now that I'm finally settled into my new digs, how I long to escape, to trade, if only for a few weeks, the maddening scenarios of my own city for another's, of my own country for a dubbed version of some foreigner's reality. But if I can't walk or swim there, at the moment I'm staying put.

For your safety. And my own.

15

An alarming lawlessness has taken hold on the streets of New Orleans, a city already infamous for its violent crime. Those in poorer neighborhoods are shooting each other right and left, at children's birthday parties, in convenience stores, or on playgrounds. Carjackings are common, especially while drivers are filling up their tanks at gas stations. A grandmother who danced every weekend at Congo Square was stabbed to death and her vehicle heisted as she unlocked her car door to leave for work one morning. Since 2019, the year before the pandemic, shootings have increased 109 percent, homicides 78 percent, and carjackings 176 percent.

In a plague, as during wars and natural disasters, when the very contours of mortality are in question, consequences disappear and the fabric of social cohesion rots. There's a sharper edge to the criminal's question: *your money or your life?*

Today at a Walgreens in the French Quarter, I ask a clerk why all of the detergents, soaps, toothpaste, shaving supplies, and cosmetics are kept locked inside shelving sealed behind plastic shields. She tells me that gangs of kids often enter to loot at will, and the clerks have no authority to stop them but can only write up reports of the incidents. The police won't arrest the shoplifters because the kids would only contract and spread the coronavirus in jail. These stolen goods are then sold to Fagin-like wholesalers, who hawk the products out of vans in distant stripmall parking lots.

As we talk, she's busy unlocking a bar of soap I want, sealed behind a plastic window. "They'll only use the money to get high on whatever they get high on. Sometimes they even ask us for a big plastic bag to put their loot in."

I'm flabbergasted. "You mean I could take all this stuff," I say, gesturing to my brimming hand basket, "and just walk out the door without paying?"

She studies the masked face of this elderly White customer to see if he's joking. "Hey, man, I didn't see nothing."

The kids, I imagine, are Black teenage boys no longer required to attend school, living with their extended families in which everyone has been laid off from their service jobs, and they themselves have lost whatever gigs they had to earn a little scratch on the side. They're probably the same fourteen year-olds who fasten bottle caps to their sneaker soles to tap dance on the sidewalks for tourist change or beat out drum solos on upended plastic buckets in front of strip joints on Bourbon Street. Now there's no structure and few male authority figures in their lives, not to mention any classes, side gigs, or tipping tourists. Mama and MawMaw are lining up at food pantries to feed the family. Why not swoop into Walgreens and waltz out with six bottles of Tide to sell to some old creep waiting in a van around the corner?

In San Francisco the Walgreens looters aren't kids but gangs of the homeless. The stores there have a similar hands-off managerial policy, which is why the cosmetics and cleaning products—of all unlikely things—are displayed in locked cubicles to keep away the unwashed sidewalk sleepers wrapped in rags. This unchecked looting is so pervasive that seventeen of the Walgreens branches throughout the city have closed down, a move that foreshadows the smash-and-grab mass robberies during the following fall. In Thomas Mann's plague-ravaged Venice, the cholera epidemic inspires a similar lawlessness. As the authorities prevaricate, issuing confusing statements, the "corruption in high places played its part, together with the suspense as to where the walking terror might strike next, to demoralize the baser elements in the city and encourage these antisocial forces which shun the light of day. . . . Gangs of men in surly mood made the streets unsafe, theft and assault were said to be frequent, even murder . . . and professional vice was rampant."

This weekend in New Orleans the windows of forty-nine cars parked at the curb were smashed in burglaries on only three streets in the nearby Tremé neighborhood. Car break-in thefts are common, and the irony is that the kids who commit these crimes first scout out the more opportune blocks in their own cars. You wouldn't expect them to walk or take the bus to batter a windshield or hijack a car, would you?

Meanwhile, as the desperation of those below boils over, our respectable representatives in Washington stall on any constructive relief in a complex game of legislative chess, each side hoping for checkmate. Money is no more than numbers on a computer screen, even as the inflationary nightmares of the Weimar Republic or post-crash Argentina flash in the rearview mirror. I have little faith that these politicians, some well-meaning progressive Democrats and others Republican corporate lackeys, will help the Walgreens looters or car-window smashers.

"A plague o' both their houses" is the resounding curse that echoes throughout the family rivalry between the Montegues and the Capulets in *Romeo and Juliet*. I'm not a team player, and as a nonpartisan outlier observing from the sidelines, I don't identify with either of these two warring houses, but with Shakespeare's tragic young lovers whose lives are destroyed by the ongoing enmity.

And both of our houses are becoming even more divided during this plague, marked by a seething populist resentment in the flyover heartland of the country and a withering condescension among educated coastal leftists. According to a recent poll by the Pew Research Center, among the Danish 72 percent feel that their country has become more unified during the pandemic, as if combating it were a collective wartime effort. In the United States, only 18 percent agree with this assessment. Some Americans choose to speak in the distancing lingo of "systemic racism" and "White privilege" to show that they're people of social conscience on the correct side. Others spew vitriolic hatred against those in any way different from themselves. Everyone is seething with grievance against their fellow citizens, the government, and history. Yet a long glance back at the pestilence-ravaged centuries, with a bird's-eye view of the poverty and suffering endured by generation after generation of frail humans on earth, asks that we spotlight only one or two scenes from *Les Miserables* to illustrate our past, present, and the prospects for our future.

16

The end.

As we approach New Year's Eve of 2020, once again I think of that precipitous cliff in time that I couldn't quite see over while pondering the Book of Revelations at age ten. That date stopped cold my childhood daydreams about an unimaginable future. I wonder if we're at the end of the beginning, over the hump of the middle, or at the beginning of the end of this plague. The various coronavirus vaccines beginning to circulate spell hope, as does the much anticipated exit of the mad king, who three weeks before the coronation of a new president still refuses to admit that he's been dethroned or make any plans to leave the palace. Yet the pestilence continues to rage among an increasingly desperate population. And it's no surprise that the two new viral hotspots are the global air hubs of Los Angeles and London. The United Kingdom is now further isolated from the world during its final week as a member of the European Union, the final act of a tragedy with unimaginable consequences. Much like isolated England, we've all become islands of mistrust, fear, confusion, anger, and denial, speaking in a cacophony of mutually unintelligible slogans.

This is the syntax of endgame.

At the stroke of midnight on New Year's Eve, as my great-grandparents' recently repaired mantelpiece clock chimes twelve, I study the winged helmet of the statue of Hermes seated next to its round dial, and gobble down twelve grapes. This is a Spanish superstition to guarantee good luck during the New Year. No matter where I happen to be in the world, I've been observing this ritual for the past forty years, ever since my first New Year's Eve in Barcelona in 1980. Except usually eating the grapes is done among much hugging, kissing, and raucous merry-making, and this is the first time I've ever eaten alone these sacred *uvas de la Nochevieja*. All bars are closed, and the city has canceled the firework displays along the riverfront to avoid attracting crowds. Police cruisers patrol the streets to break up any private parties or clusters of sidewalk revelers. I wasn't able to entice friends of any nationality to "eat the grapes" with me. They expressed fear of indoor gatherings or the supposedly "severe storms" expected at midnight, a torrential rain that never arrived. My skeptical streak suspects the weather casters made up the threatening storms to keep people at home.

I stand at my front door, a flute of Spanish champagne in hand, and greet the few straggling young people in sparkly cardboard top hats who stagger past, probably on the way back to their Airbnbs. As usual, they seem more interested in documenting the experience by taking selfies than in actually living it. I stand back to observe the strangeness of this time and place, taking my own mental selfie of this eerie *Twilight Zone* episode, the first moments of 2021. This is the most foreign country I've ever visited, even though I'm only six blocks away from the Bourbon Street house where my great-grandmother Landry grew up with the same clock that just chimed midnight. As the clock struck the hours, there the winged statue of Hermes, much like the ebony clock in Poe's "The Masque of the Red Death," stood witness as four of her six siblings lay dying of yellow fever during the 1880s.

Tonight most of us are at home, not dying.

This moment between dying and not dying is punctuated by a hoarse exclamation from a straggling passerby: "Happy New Year!" I lift my flute, we wave, and then I swing shut my front door on what was supposed to be our long-awaited liberation: the opening.

Part III

Endgame

Hamm: *I love the old questions.*
(With fervor.)
Ah the old questions, the old answers,
there's nothing like them!

—Samuel Beckett, *Endgame*

1

On the last day of Christmas, which we celebrate in New Orleans as Twelfth Night, this year I wasn't eating king cake or exchanging gifts. I was glued to the television, along with most other Americans, watching as state representatives in the nation's Capitol cowered on the floor while Trump's armed mob of shouting louts invaded their congressional chamber, interrupting Congress's certification of the electoral college's presidential vote. I couldn't believe my eyes as a horned, half-naked man in face paint stepped up onto the rostrum of House Speaker Nancy Pelosi. He wouldn't have looked out of place here at Carnival nor during some sixties acid fest in San Francisco, but what was he doing among Confederate flags and club-waving hordes in the august sanctum of our democracy?

This spectacle jolted me back to a similar moment in Spain more than thirty years ago, one that rattled me at the time and unnerved the Spanish for a generation. On that occasion, a drunken army colonel had stood at the speaker's podium during a presidential election in the Palacio de las Cortes in Madrid and fired shots into the air, shouting *todos al suelo,* or "everyoneon the ground." Whether incited by a crazed colonel or a defeated president who refuses to leave office, how fragile the stately marble pillars of democracy suddenly can appear.

And we should never take their permanence for granted again.

During my first attempted coup d'état, I didn't even have a radio, much less a television. On the evening of February 23, 1981, while a Fulbright professor of North American Studies at the Universidad Central de Barcelona, I was teaching a class on Walt Whitman. Suddenly a group of uniformed janitors burst into the classroom, insisting that we leave immediately.

"Everything is normal again. The Fascists are back in power," they announced, faces flushed with booze. "Everyone go home until further notice."

Needless to say, I was shocked that these taciturn watchmen, usu-ally perched inside of glass security booths in the university patios, were invading my class. But my fourth-year philology students knew what it meant. They'd grown up under the iron fist of Generalissimo Francisco Franco, dead for only seven years, and realized how shaky the present transition to democracy was. They communicated the gravity of the situation to me in English as we marched out under the stern glares of the gloating *bedeles*.

Walking the few blocks home, as I shouldered past stunned pe-destrians scampering down Las Ramblas, I couldn't believe what was happening. My American girlfriend, still in stage makeup, soon rushed back to our apartment. Maureen was a dancer who had been perform-ing in a musical comedy version of the Noah story, *El diluvio que viene* (based on the novel *After Me the Deluge*), in a theater on the Avenida del Paralelo, Barcelona's answer to Broadway. Armed civil guards had interrupted the show, emptying the theater with the same explanation.

In the blink of an eye, everything had changed.

Shaking our heads in disbelief, we stood at the railing of one of our seven balconies over the Calle Elisabets, watching the street empty. Would we have to pack our bags and leave the country?

We'd made friends with the grandfatherly proprietor of a milk shop on the building's first floor, so we went down to ask the *lechero* what the hell was going on. Gray head bowed, he sat slumped next to his radio, muttering under his breath.

"How could this be happening?" he kept repeating. "And the rest of the military is behind him!"

He told us that a lieutenant colonel named Antonio Tejero had taken over the speaker's podium in the Spanish parliament in Madrid, interrupting a congressional vote to elect a new president, the Democratic candidate Leopoldo Calvo-Sotelo. Waving a pistol, Tejero commanded that the now kidnapped representatives get down on the floor, shouting that the election was canceled and the Fascist Party again in power. At that moment, tanks commandeered by two thousand soldiers were rumbling through the streets of Valencia, and a national military coup d'état had been declared.

The Catalan milkman explained that he'd been a Republican during the Civil War, fighting the Fascists. Even though a bomb had blown off his leg—he rolled up a pant cuff to show us the prosthetic limb—he kept a wooden club under the counter that he was now brandishing at the stentorian voice on the state-run radio station, announcing the coup as definitive. He was preparing to limp two blocks to Las Ramblas to fight the bastards again. In his twitching face, he was reliving the horror of the war, when one half of Spain invaded the other half, both sides mercilessly slaughtering each other.

Of course, during my two years in Barcelona I'd heard a lot about the four decades of Franco's rule and the civil war, but had no idea what was happening at the moment. We were renting the elegant, if threadbare, apartment of a Catalan poet, Père Rovira, who suddenly showed up at the front door. Père, who had been part of the youthful resistance to Franco, explained to us the seriousness of the coup d'état as he packed a suitcase of his papers related to the anti-Fascist underground. He planned to cross the border into France in the morning. He assured me that, as a Fulbright professor, I'd probably be all right, since Franco had always counted on the staunch support of the American State Department. Yet I certainly didn't want to play along with the Fascists.

Maureen and I stayed up most of that fretful night, pacing the tile floors from balcony to balcony to stare out over the eerily deserted street. We had no telephone, so we couldn't call friends either in Barcelona or abroad to confirm what was happening. Then the light in the milkman's shop went out, breaking our news connection to the world.

At dawn that morning, we later heard, King Juan Carlos I appeared on television to denounce Tejero, the military insurrectionists, and the attempted coup, reaffirming his support for the constitution drawn up three years earlier. In a short, forceful speech, he decreed from the Palacio Real that Spain would continue its transition to democracy. This was followed by the national anthem and an image of the Spanish flag.

Period.

The coup d'état was over.

Later that day the front pages of *El País* and *La Vanguardia* stacked in the newspaper kiosks along Las Ramblas recounted the unsettling story of the drunken soldiers and their botched takeover of the government. The sun rose on a new day in Spain, but only we foreigners believed it. Life appeared to return to normal, but the Spaniards' faith in the authority and continuity of a new-born democracy was badly shaken after witnessing in one stressful night how easily the flickering candle of their freedom could be blown out.

Remembering this failed coup in Spain, I'd been predicting some crazed last-minute attempt by Trump to maintain power. Like Franco during his dictatorship, the president was a cult figure, and populist icons don't step down gracefully from their pedestals. I'd been recounting my prophecies to friends while assuring them that at least, unlike under Franco, the military wasn't behind him, especially after he called war veterans "losers and suckers." I pegged Trump as a delusional sociopath the minute he rode down that escalator to declare his candidacy and knew that such manic narcissists never give up. Yet recently I had little idea what form his Adderall-addled attempts would take. I suspected that before being forced from office he'd launch a nuclear war with Iran, which he did propose yet the State Department rejected. That he might declare martial law, or a state of siege, also had crossed my mind, an idea that the "suckers and losers" in the military shot down.

What I hadn't taken into account was the power of the social media sites by which Trump had magnetized his extremist followers, the various platforms of Twitter or Fritter, Facebook or Assbook—whatever they're called. That world is as alien to me as Mars, as are the conspiratorial caverns created by the president's Rasputin, Alex Jones, through which Trump first recruited his fanatic base. Evidently, it was Jones who dreamed up, among other delirious theories, Trutherism (the massacre at Sandy Hook was staged), Birtherism (Obama was born in Kenya), and Pizzagate (Hillary Clinton is a Satanic pedophile working out of a pizza parlor's basement). These wacky conspiracy theorists thriving on the dark web, initiates in Trump's paranoid cult, were evidently among those who stormed Congress. Later we learned that the bare-chested, horned creature who stood at Pelosi's podium was a self-styled shaman in the QAnon movement, whose dogmas include Trutherism, Birtherism, and Pizzagate.

Don't get me wrong. I'm a fiction writer and love a good lie, as long as the story remains anchored in the artistic realm of the imagination. And I don't understand the addiction to social media news, with its lack of gatekeepers and disregard for fact-checking. Living in downtown New Orleans, there's always enough of a commotion going on around me that I don't need to thumb a chunk of electronic plastic to simulate either connection or communication. So little did I suspect that almost a month before what we celebrate here as Twelfth Night (what the French call *la fête des Rois* and the Spanish *Reyes)*, sweatshirts were being sold on the dark web with slogans announcing "MAGA Civil War—January 6."

The riot in congress was no flash mob, but an elaborately orchestrated national gathering, like some nutty trade convention. Flights were booked, hotel rooms reserved. During this dreary winter of the pandemic, I suppose that isolated people whose only reality is scrolling through a cell phone, with no king cakes or Carnival to look forward to, long for something real. And in a cartoonish civil war they can flesh out an action-comic version of their most conspiratorial fantasies. Good Boy Scouts, these insurrectionists came prepared with gas masks, pipe bombs, handcuff zipties, climbing equipment, and pistols. In the rowdy spirit of a NASCAR race or a tailgate party, they wanted their team to win. We still wonder how many uniformed congressional guards, in cahoots with the insurrectionists like those janitors who emptied my classroom in Barcelona, were on their side, allowing them to pour into the capitol building. At least twenty of them were former soldiers, employing military jargon to organize the rioting.

Yet this wasn't a backslapping sporting event, scouting jamboree, or army maneuver, but an attempted coup d'état.

Are Americans so divorced from reality that we can't tell the difference?

Unlike the Spanish, we don't have a king to maintain civil order: the teacher who walks into an unruly schoolyard, clapping her hands. Yet what we do have is a constitution drafted more than two centuries ago. We Americans may not all believe in the same God, but we do have a legal bible whose parchment pages we can study. We have that, along with 27,000 National Guardsmen now patrolling Washington, DC, to enforce it. Trump finally got his state of siege, but one to keep his own followers at bay.

Many now predict that when the restrictions of the coronavirus pandemic are lifted, another Roaring Twenties will blossom, as after the end of the deadly influenza epidemic in 1918. Leaving behind the virtual tedium of Zoom, they say, we'll twenty-three-skidoo back together to kick up our heels, booty to booty.

And in this same spirit, a most remarkable era took place in Spain after the attempted coup of 1981. Under Franco, young Spaniards never experienced anything like our explosive sixties or the *soixante-huit* rebellion of the French, and they suddenly made up for lost time with a vengeance. The failed coup sparked the inception of the *movida madrileña*, that libidinous decade best captured in the wacky early films of Pedro Almodóvar, filled with defiant punk rock, drugs, gays, drag queens, outré fashions, and joyous all-night outpourings of outrageousness onto the streets of Madrid. Most elements of this scene were still illegal, but nobody cared. They lived in a democracy and, as conflictive as that could get, had a constitution that evidently could stand the test of time.

I can feel it in my bones. During an endless pandemic, and after four years of Trump's lunacy crowned by this failed coup, we're much like the Spanish in the early eighties, on the brink of a new era. Before I moved back to Spain in 1989, I visited Madrid often. San Francisco, where I lived at the time, was drying up, choked to death by Reaganomics, AIDS, real estate, yuppies, and political correctness. The thirst that drew me back is best illustrated in a scene in Almodóvar's *Women on the Verge of a Nervous Breakdown*, when a frazzled Carmen Maura stumbles through the late-night streets of Madrid, which the sanitation crews are hosing down. She marches straight into the powerful blast of water from a hose nozzle and, dripping wet, raises her hands to the sky, shouting "*Régame, régame.*"

Water me, water me.

After pandemics and coups, dictators and failed governments: *el diluvio que viene*, or the deluge to come.

2

"We've become a Beckett play." In *Year of the Monkey*, Patti Smith quotes her dying friend, the playwright Sam Shepard, struggling with her to finish his final work. "I imagine us rooted in our place at the kitchen table," Smith writes, "each of us dwelling in a barrel with a tin lid . . . as if we are alone, not alone together but each alone, not disturbing the aura of the other's aloneness."

This is an apt description of the new lockdown in mid-January. Rumors circulate that Carnival may be canceled. In New Orleans we're back in a modified Phase I of health mandates, and the lists of regulations I receive from the gym and hairdresser are discouraging. At the gym, face masks are required except while swimming or showering, yet even while naked drying off in the locker room. At the hairdresser, you make an appointment as usual, but now have to telephone from the street, waiting outside in the cold or rain until the previous client has left. I refuse to pay a lot of money to be so uptight, especially in places where I used to go to relax.

Most of us are not fully alive yet not dying. We communicate with each other like Nagg and Nell in Samuel Beckett's terse existentialist play *Endgame*, in which the protagonist Hamm keeps his toothless parents barely alive in adjoining lidded barrels. Today, moving vans are parked in front of the White House, state capitols are in military lockdown to discourage further insurrections, stimulus checks haven't arrived, and coronavirus vaccine distribution is in disarray. The websites to schedule vaccine appointments have crashed and the phone lines to unemployment offices are eternally busy. The states blame the federal government, and the feds blame the states.

Godot has come and gone, and we're still on hold, waiting.

Today, this old man in a barrel is trying to decide whether it's worth the effort to shave. The winter sky darkens before I've fully woken up. I sleep as much as possible, because my dreams, much more exciting than my daily life, are often multilingual excursions through Spain, France, Latin America, and Asia, where in wild plot twists I meet up with old friends. In the waking world, people inside of their barrels are as testy and disagreeable as Beckett characters. Nothing works right: the government, unemployment compensation, the stimulus checks, the vaccine rollout, down to the most mundane level. The stores are out of what we want.

"Distribution problems," the managers say.

This is what happens when the personal desperation of pestilence crashes into the anonymous algorithms of automation. There's a website for everything, but nobody to contact who can straighten anything out. The result is chaos.

I write this on the eve of the inauguration of a new president, one who offers a soothing message of empathy, inclusion, and unity. I think of Joe Biden as President Xanax, a much welcome change from President Adderall. Yet the national Capitol, along with the grounds of the fifty state capitols, is guarded as if preparing for an attack by a foreign enemy.

The bayonets and camouflage are real, the stars and stripes virtual.

And tucked inside our barrels of social distance, we're each sticking our heads out like one of Beckett's geezers begging for a biscuit, meanwhile guarding a hidden sugar plum to get us through the worst of winter.

3

First it was a writer friend in New Orleans who contracted a terminal sepsis, then an artist friend in Florida with the sudden onset of dementia, then a bookseller friend who lived for decades in the hectic French Quarter and, not long after moving to more sedate Uptown, died of a heart attack, and finally my old poet friend Lawrence Ferlinghetti in San Francisco. What these friends have in common, besides having been guiding lights during much of my life, is that they were in their eighties or older and previously vibrant, healthy people, who for the past year had been socially isolating to avoid contracting the coronavirus. Lawrence, of course, was housebound at 101 years old, but previously accustomed to receiving a steady stream of visitors stomping up the steps to his North Beach apartment. Older people tend to thrive on social activity and wither in solitude. None of these friends contracted the virus, yet each slid into an accelerated decline because, facing each new day inside their four walls, they found their lives emptied of friends and family, like Beckett characters living in barrels.

Was it worth it, to rigorously follow public health mandates only to sicken and die of one condition and not another?

I don't know. At the moment I'm too busy listening to the guitar of my imagination. But as for the chasm between what public health officials call their "science" and lockdown resistors insist is their "freedom," I can only quote Alistair Cooke, speaking on another subject: "The issues are so complex that the only people who make me mad are those who think they have all the answers."

In "The Costs of Prudentialism" in the *American Scholar*, the epidemiologist Philip Alcabes writes that during past decades "the institution of public health, an instrument of social engineering that had once built toilets and sewerage systems, inspected food for purity, fortified or supplemented foodstuffs with vitamins and minerals to stave off deficiency diseases, cleaned the air and water, and promoted universal prenatal care . . . [has been] descending into the role of mere advice giver." He draws a dichotomy between public health as collective infrastructure and as a mere adviser on prudent individual behavior, what he calls "prudentialism." In other words, the public works engineer who constructs projects for the health of society at large versus the strict schoolmarm who elicits eye rolls from the back of the classroom. In this sense, the drinking water tragedy in Flint, Michigan, is a major failure of what should be public health, while banning the sale of large bottles of sweetened soda is what Alcabes brands as "prudentialism." He argues that "the framework of American medicine has shifted away from remedying social ills to demanding personal propriety."

In other words, it has become part of the nanny-state.

Alcabes gets to the heart of the mask-wearing debate by comparing individuals' reactions to the AIDS and coronavirus pandemics. I well remember that during the eighties in San Francisco the debate about AIDS was as fiery as the one now about personal prevention practices. At the time I agreed that gay bathhouses should be closed as incubators of the disease, a controversy of much heated crossfire in the press. But it never would have occurred to me to criticize my own friends' sexual choices, some of which were pretty bad. And so they died.

Despite all of the self-righteous preaching, little progress was made in combating the epidemic until the Gay Men's Health Clinic movement emerged as a radical alternative to public health, protesting for accelerated antiviral drug approval and distribution. Sensible as it once seemed, Alcabes understands that advising certain gay men to abandon their sexual promiscuity threatened their very identity, what they considered their self-defining freedom. In the same way, many lockdown protestors now resist the finger-wagging public health mandates about how to celebrate Thanksgiving and Christmas, which they feel encroach on their family identities.

Alcabes points out that the admonitions back then not to screw around, and the warnings these days to practice social distancing, don't constitute real public health. Sound as the preventive advice may be, public health consists in coordinating reliable testing, contact tracing, as well as developing and distributing vaccines or antiviral treatments. And during both epidemics, American public health has failed miserably. In short, the prudential message has been *don't be stupid*: of course people should wear condoms in bed and face masks in public. But somehow the viruses may get us in ways we never expected. Condoms can break, lovers cheat, and partners lie. Within large households, a child can infect a grandmother, or harried grocery clerks can spread the virus to their whole families. And it's the real role of public health to take collective action to remedy the tidal waves of these inevitable infections. Needless to say, eat right. But whether you shop for kale at Whole Foods or frozen pizza at Seven-Eleven, you may get sick unless the food you buy is first inspected for bacterial contaminates, and only the infrastructure of public health can accomplish this.

Public health's mission should be to allow us the security to make these personal choices, whether prudent or bone-headed, not to make them for us.

So in spite of the well-intentioned, if conflicting, advice given during the present pandemic, public health institutions have failed to stop the coronavirus. At the moment, the great debate among health experts is whether to wear only one face mask or two. Some argue for three. I'm not listening, because these experts aren't doing their real jobs: the infrastructures for testing, contact tracing, and vaccinations remain chaotic and woefully inadequate.

I've never been tested because, as a pedestrian with no car, there are no walk-up testing sites in my neighborhood, the densely inhabited heart of downtown New Orleans. Evidently, to be tested people have to visit some drive-through strip mall miles away to wait in line for hours in their vehicles. I regularly walk to the French Quarter Walgreens to refill my prescriptions. Yet when I ask about access to coronavirus testing or the vaccine at the drugstore, Mr. Gerald, the pharmacist, sadly shakes his graying head of hair, as if to say *dream on, baby.*

4

I've spent the past week conspiring with other septuagenarians about where to find the vaccine, as if we were a bunch of junkies trying to score their next fix before they get sick. This is to the soundtrack of Lou Reed's sinister lyrics about "waiting for my man." Like the junkies' dealer, our man never shows up on the expected corners. We are constantly disappointed, then angry. First Oschsner Hospital cancels my appointment for last week, citing a lack of reliable supply. Then Touro Hospital calls to postpone until mid-March an appointment I made for yesterday, January 29.

But I score anyway.

After torturing myself for two hours on the LSU Healthcare Network website, stymied time and again by commands to sign my name online—which I have no idea how to do—or to scan my state ID and insurance cards into the application, another digital maneuver that baffles me. The irony is that this first round of vaccines is limited to those seventy years or older, hardly the most tech savvy demographic in the world. Which public health official came up with this brilliant plan of algorithms for the elderly? Somehow or other I make it through the tedious registration protocols, and then a confirmation pops up with an actual phone number on it. The lady I speak with couldn't be sweeter or more helpful, and I wonder why I couldn't have spoken with her in the first place.

I excitedly call friends hanging on canceled or postponed vaccine appointments. I've found "my man, twenty-six dollars in my hand." Three of my contacts make appointments for the next day, but I wait another two days to see if this miracle will actually materialize.

And it does, functioning as public health should.

The Louisiana State University Medical Center is an expansive complex of buildings that occupies thirty-square blocks of downtown New Orleans. Its disruptive construction was a political boondoggle for then governor Bobby Jindal, a scrawny Punjabi version of Donald Trump, and was a wastefully foolish mistake. At this same time the graceful thirties-era Charity Hospital sat moldering, trusted by generations of locals yet abandoned after Hurricane Katrina. To construct this new Dallas-like complex, miles of traditional New Orleans architecture were demolished, displacing whole neighborhoods of people who had returned home after Hurricane Katrina to rebuild their flooded nineteenth-century houses. It's now a nightmarish reincarnation of Robert Moses's vision of sixties-era urban renewal, a maze of glass-walled and poured concrete buildings that replaced a huge swath of this city's cultural and architectural heritage.

I always swore that I'd never set foot inside.

But desperate vaccine junkie that I am, if that's the street corner where "my man" is dealing, I go. I soon find out that the hospital has an extensive supply of the Pfizer vaccine, distributed by the federal government directly to the states, because as a state-sponsored institution, you can guess where it landed. So while private hospitals are scrimping along as best they can, the real stash goes to "my man," Louisiana State University.

The cavernous first floor of the building where the injections are given is well staffed, probably by medical school residents and nursing students, and the process efficiently organized. I hand a lady seated at a table a paper printout of the form that took me hours to complete online, an application that would have taken two minutes to fill out on the spot. As analog as I am, I sign it by hand. I show her my state ID and then perform a lithe strip tease, shedding winter gear down to a short-sleeved shirt that reveals a bare arm.

It's over in ten seconds.

Then for fifteen minutes I sit on a socially distanced folding chair facing a plateglass wall, starring at a screen that scrolls through data about the COVID-19 vaccine. Inside the soaring dome of this medical space station, I feel like a human abducted by aliens being indoctrinated in a science fiction movie. Or like I'd just received Communion in some futuristic Mass celebrated in an airport departure lounge. This is a reverent moment of silent contrition for my pandemic sins, such as when the imp of the perverse emerged during my angry confrontation with the hand-sanitizer cop at the grocery store or my impatience in dealing with student writers anxious about returning to in-person workshops. *Mea culpa mea maxima culpa.*

I should be kneeling, forehead in my hands.

Because now I'm saved, right?

Instead, I ask a lady seated at an exit table to call a taxi to take me home. True, I have a new Android cell phone in my shoulder bag, but it confuses me and this cranky septuagenarian doesn't feel like fooling with any more frustrating screens and buttons.

Once home, my upper arm aches a bit, and the apartment feels cold as a meat freezer. I crank up the heat, then an old friend drops by for a glass of wine as I sit in my great-grandmother's rocking chair with a Guatemalan wool blanket draped over my lap. By the time my friend leaves, I'm broiling.

An achy upper arm. Chills and fever. I've been warned.

I fall asleep for nine hours, forgetting even to brush my teeth.

Waking the next day I feel normal. I slip on my face mask as I enter a supermarket. I may be vaccinated—thank you, Jesus—but the world is still on fire, the pandemic raging. I edge too close to a young woman in the vegetable aisle and she scurries away, as if I were the skeletal Grim Reaper himself swinging my scythe. In apology, I want to sputter *sic transit gloria mundi, honey.*

And what a sick transit it has been.

5

Oddly enough, the best Mardi Gras ever was during the Carnival season of 2006, six months after the massive destruction wrought by Hurricane Katrina. At the time, many New Orleanians were rebuilding their flooded houses, out of work, and living in trailers. Streets were lined with boarded-up shop windows and mountains of storm debris. Still in shock, we were angry at the government's failure to help us, but remained defiant, high-spirited, and hell-bent to rebuild the city on our own.

That year a great debate erupted about whether to cancel Carnival, since so many locals were marooned out of state, camping out on relatives' couches. The world had been watching for months as the horrors of the aftermath unfolded, so few tourists were booking flights or hotel rooms to our mold-infested disaster zone. But we surviving residents insisted, and once it was decided to move forward with the Carnival celebrations, the scarcity of tourists was what made the season so special for locals.

It was a Mardi Gras for us—the survivors—not for them, the gawkers.

During the satiric parades, we howled at the locally themed jokes brandished on floats about FEMA, house trailers, roofing tarps, Bush, Heck-of-a-Job-Brownie, the National Guard, and dysfunctional City Hall. As a damaged community, at that particular moment what we needed was the polar opposite of social distancing: to hug each other, drink, cavort, laugh, and reinforce our determination to survive.

The words were on everyone's lips: "Best Carnival ever!"

In spite of the odds, we were back home and together.

This pandemic year, on the other hand, has been the worst Carnival ever, the Mardi Gras-that-wasn't.

At first the mayor, LaToyota Can't Tell, welcomed visitors with open arms to live it up on our picturesque streets, delivering a sly we-need-the-business come on. And then a video circulated of crowds herding together one Saturday night in drunken abandon on the Bourbon Street strip-joint mall. Once again she had to face the crossfire between competing pressures from the public health establishment and the hospitality industry. Still smarting from the national criticism about how she blindly proceeded with the 2020 Carnival season that seeded the city with coronavirus, this year she canceled the parades, abruptly closed every bar in the city for the peak six days of the holiday, and locked down the French Quarter as if it were as toxic as Chernobyl. Large areas were fenced off under the overpass on Claiborne Avenue, the traditional stomping grounds of the Mardi Gras Indians since long before the oppressive freeway trashed the area during the urban renewal sixties. And she accomplished what even dour Presidents Harding, Coolidge, and Hoover couldn't manage during the thirteen bootleg-soaked years of Prohibition. Not only were the bars closed citywide, but to-go drinks and package liquor sales prohibited in the French Quarter.

For six days I couldn't buy a bottle of wine in my own neighborhood.

And this was during Carnival.

In spite of the multiple lockdown restrictions, my friends and I planned to costume anyway, to roam the French Quarter streets on Fat Tuesday with hip flasks tucked under feathers and fringe. You can't cancel the historically Catholic holiday of Shrove Tuesday, we insisted, which initiates the Lenten season on Ash Wednesday. And unlike some weenie roast spoiled by rain, you can't postpone it, as some people suggested, anymore than you can postpone Christmas or Easter for better weather in May. The church calendar doesn't work that way, and this ancestral culture has been in our blood for centuries.

As we were reminded after Katrina, the midwinter festival of Mardi Gras is fiercely celebrated not because everything is so wonderful but in spite of everything that isn't. It's a day to slip those aching personal tragedies into our back pockets, and the more woes we need to forget, the more delirious the fun. "Your joy is your sorrow unmasked," as Kahlil Gibran writes. "The deeper that sorrow carves into your being, the more joy you can contain." This year the masked holiday has been canceled, or rather a jester's mask changed for a medical face mask, our joy for our sorrow.

Some locals tried to refashion this most pedestrian of raucous street parties into a drive-through event. Instead of standing shoulder to shoulder watching the parades of floats wind through the streets, residents were encouraged to use Carnival themes to decorate the fronts of their homes, so people could drive past as if admiring Christmas light displays. They christened this "Yardi Gras." I find it depressing how Americans instinctively turn to their machines and devices when their reality is challenged, such as staging a drive-through Carnival or a Zoom birthday party.

Better than nothing, you say?

When a romance sours, you may reach for a battery-powered blow-up doll, but please don't call it love. Lost love is a poignant emotion, the theme of much of our greatest art, one that I'd prefer to experience in its passionate depths rather than hit a keyboard or flick on a switch in its place. Every major setback doesn't merit a mechanical or digital solution, especially when the missing ingredient is other people. Allowing ourselves to feel loss is part of being fully human, as Elizabeth Bishop observes in her villanelle "One Art": "The art of losing's not too hard to master / thought it may look like (*Write it!*) like disaster."

As it turns out, this blow-up doll of a Mardi-Gras-that-wasn't has been deep-sixed by the Arctic blast of frigid weather sweeping across the country this week, the same one that has frozen the neighboring Lone Star State. The temperature on Mardi Gras morning is 25 degrees, and it never rises past a breezy 32 all day, maintaining a wind chill factor of 17 degrees. I haul out my box of Carnival treasures from years past and wear a pearl crown inside, but under the frigid, leaden sky don't stick my nose outdoors all day. A handful of shivering friends drop by to raise a glass of champagne and munch on king cake, but that's it.

The freezing temperatures would have been enough to socially distance us, so we don't need all of the fencing, roadblocks, and party-pooping health strictures to keep us close to the heaters inside. The coldest Mardi Gras on record, it's a grim day for a street celebration and an even worse one for the voracious coronavirus. Most of its potential victims are huddled indoors, far away from its spiked crowns.

For Lent this year I've decided to give up Lent itself, to put this whole ashen year behind me. Any more deliberate sacrifice or penitence on my part seems beside the point. On the day after Ash Wednesday, I end the Mardi-Gras-week-that-wasn't with a second dose of the vaccine at LSU, and spend most of the post-Carnival weekend in bed, arm aching, covered with blankets to ward off both the Pfizer chills inside my body and the more unrelenting cold outside.

After taking more than a half a million American lives, the pandemic is still raging, and now slick Arctic ice has blanketed the usually verdant and temperate South. This week nature is having its vengeful way with us, blowing our fancy prancing to smithereens, along with those flimsy cardboard crowns and sugary king cakes.

6

Evidently the United States isn't the only place embroiled in the chaos of the vaccine roll out. Actually, in this country the vaccine is being distributed three times faster than in the European Union. In Spain the situation is particularly a mess. Patricia, my good friend from Madrid, calls to tell me that she's spending the month of March in her native Dallas to finally receive both doses of the vaccine. She has lived in Madrid since the seventies, where she worked as the American program officer of the Spanish Fulbright Commission, which was where we met during my first teaching fellowship in 1979. She was in charge of orienting the American grantees and overseeing their university posts and research in Spain. She's held dual nationality for forty years and, although now retired, had one of most prestigious positions that a naturalized citizen can achieve in that now very modern country.

Yet even she can't get the vaccine.

"They had me scheduled for late June," she tells me, "and I finally lost patience. You need to know a politician or someone who works in the government to get it any sooner."

This reflects the Spanish system of *enchufre*, which means that the only way to get anything—a job, promotion, appointment, or grant— is through a personal connection, or who you know. Common enough in New Orleans, I instinctively understand this attitude, which must be part of our Spanish cultural legacy, like animated street life and shouting in crowded restaurants. Growing up, whenever anyone in my family encountered a bureaucratic snafu, they immediately asked each other, "Who do we know who works in that office?"

Obviously Patricia doesn't know anyone in the Spanish Ministry of Health because, as a seventy-year-old Spanish citizen, she should have been among the first in line for the vaccine. During my ten years living in Spain, I found the government-run public medical system to be both efficient and accessible. The best part is that it's free, both for citizens and foreigners alike. Although you can count me as a committed European-style socialist when it comes to education and medical care, I never had to wait in a line with millions of people for a life-saving shot.

Not that Patricia has found the vaccine distribution any easier to maneuver in Dallas. She came only because her brother knew of an easily available vaccination site at the Christus St. Michael Health Center, a Catholic mission in Texarkana.

"So my brother drove me to the mission last week for my first shot," she says, obviously relieved, "but a two-hour-forty-minute drive is a lot easier than waiting four months to get the vaccination in Madrid, where my appointment can be postponed at any moment. There the situation is so frustrating that it was worth catching a really expensive international flight, packed to the roof, by the way. And I had to have a COVID test three days before boarding, and then have to get another one three days before I return. Yet after all that rigmarole, no alcohol is served, and no butter with the bread."

This happens to be the seventy-fifth anniversary of the Fulbright Commission, during which both here and around the world many ballyhooed events have been set up to celebrate the success of this cultural exchange program, an educational parallel to the Peace Corps. But an administrative veteran of this laudable commission can't find a way to be vaccinated in her adopted European country, one with an excellent public health system.

What's wrong with this picture?

And for those who have no choice at this moment but to catch a pricey international flight, after having cotton swabs jammed up their noses, why can't they be served a glass of wine and butter with their bread?

7

"I don't know."

That's been my automatic response to every question I've been asked during the past year. Will I conduct another writing workshop this spring? Will New Orleans ever recover from the pandemic? Am I glad that I moved back to the French Quarter? Will Donald Trump be defeated in the November elections? Do I think that face masks really prevent coronavirus infections? Have I ever suffered any symptoms of the virus? Would I be tested if given the chance? Will I ever fly again? Will I return to swim at my health club?

Do I think I might die of this thing?

Today is March 16, 2021, and a calendar year has passed since my life was abruptly shut down on this same date in 2020, when my classes were canceled, the gym closed, bus service reduced, and grocery shelves emptied. And I still don't know.

True, we now have a new president, I've been recently vaccinated, and because of a low infection and death rate, New Orleans is now within the convoluted parameters of a "modified Phase III," the details of which remain vague. Live music is permitted inside clubs, but the limited audience must be seated at tables, where they can neither mingle nor dance. So there are grounds for hope, even as the medical experts threaten us with more lockdowns if we get too feisty and, say, kick up our heels. As a new wave of infections threatens Europe, St. Patrick's Day crowds clog the sidewalks of the Quarter while images flash across the TV screen of boisterous hordes of college students on spring break whooping it up at the beach in Florida.

The more I learn, the less I know. And so I've come to trust the spokespeople who share my unsettling doubt.

I only pay attention to public health statements about the coronavirus prefaced by a phrase such as "we don't know, but . . ." or "although we're not sure, there's evidence that . . . ." "Science" has been proven so wrong during the past year in its understanding of this deviously mysterious illness that only some degree of investigative humility inspires my faith. Gone is that era early in the pandemic when epidemiologists could capture my confidence by asserting their firm conclusions gathered from research, "following the science," as they put it.

Then we were expected to shut up, listen, and obey. Now there are more questions than answers, and I respect those scientists who admit it.

New areas of doubt make my head spin, such as:

The unreliability of contradictory results from different tests.

The number and origins of the new variants, now estimated to be in the thousands.

The ongoing mutation of the virus within seriously ill patients.

"Long-haulers," or those infected who were never hospitalized but continue to suffer bizarre aftereffects from the virus long after recovery.

"Long COVID" in young children, who at first weren't considered susceptible to falling ill.

Those infected who suddenly drop dead without showing any previous symptoms.

The brain lesions discovered during autopsies of those who have died of COVID-19.

How the vaccinated, although protected themselves, can still spread infection.

The range of international variants from which the vaccination currently keeps us safe.

The vaccine is supposed to shield us from fatal infection for the rest of our lives— but no, wait a minute—this just in: perhaps for only three to six months.

For a year now we've heard the unrelenting mantra to maintain a "social distancing" of six feet from others. Waiting in store lines, we religiously station ourselves at that distance within circles stenciled on the floor like stage markings. Yet now a new study from Harvard finds that the infection rate between elementary school students seated at desks six feet and three feet apart is negligible. As catechistic conceptions about the pandemic are being reexamined, our faith is shaken. It's as if new evidence suggests that Jesus didn't really walk on water, but sank. Or did he float? Like Hamm in Beckett's play *Endgame*, we've come to relish the old questions and the old answers.

A growing consensus is that we'll have to receive a booster vaccination every year to prevent falling ill with one of the rapidly multiplying variants, much like the annual flu shot advised for the same reason. Considering the confusing inaccessibility surrounding the initial roll out of the vaccine, and the difficulty in convincing many people to get it, this could prove an enormous undertaking. Perhaps in the far distant future the vaccine could be combined with the flu shot and, dropping by our neighborhood pharmacies as we do now, it could become a casual yearly ritual.

Yet much like wearing face masks, the degree to which the vaccine has become politicized indicates a crescendo of popular distrust of public health. Forty-seven percent of those who voted for Donald Trump are now refusing to be vaccinated, and he lost the presidential election by a narrow margin. In several paranoid fantasies I've heard, straight out of the creepy alien invasion scenarios of science fiction movies, people claim that these sneaky shots are the "mark of the beast," meant to modify our DNA or to slip a computer chip into our bodies that would turn us unto into zombies brainwashed by IT corporations. Several Catholic priests have objected that the vaccine is manufactured from research using aborted fetuses, and a Muslim cleric has warned that it will turn people gay.

This is the post-truth world in which we now live.

Although I haven't had the flu in twenty years, and so forgo the flu shot offered every year at my neighborhood Walgreens, I'm grateful that I received the polio and smallpox vaccines as a child, as well as the vaccines that kept me healthy while traveling through the subtropics, and would have taken an AIDS vaccine in a snap, had one been developed. I acknowledge that medical science has gotten many things wrong over the decades—especially during the polio and AIDS epidemics that I survived—but I'm no fool. Skepticism may be in order, but delusion and denial are unsettling, especially when the results of political manipulation. The anti-vaxers can go their defiant way, if their suspicions make them feel like iconoclastic antiheroes, but they will prolong this pandemic by months, even years.

Every year in New Orleans, from June through October, we sit glued to the weather reports about approaching hurricanes that might enter the Gulf of Mexico. When one does, the newscasters illustrate its possible path inside of tentative triangles, according to various meteorological models. They call this the "cone of uncertainty." We pay rapt attention to their hazy predictions—while one hand packs a suitcase as the other clutches a flashlight—because they admit that, at the moment, they don't know. Experts should be applauded when they confess what they simply don't know. Oddly enough, it inspires confidence.

Should these meteorologists hazard a dire warning only for us to awake on the dreaded day to blue skies and balmy weather, we won't trust future storm scares and will make no preparations, even as a killer hurricane like Katrina shifts paths to barrel down on us. We maintain faith in the weather reports so long as the newscasters, one eyebrow cocked, acknowledge their uncertainties. Should they radiate certainty and be wrong too often, we go about our business at our own peril, tuning out and pretending the real threat is slim.

During this year of the pandemic, we have learned to live within a similar cone of uncertainty, hearing this report yesterday, a contradictory one today, yet remaining alert and shouldering on. Grouchy Fauci was right about one thing: this has been a long, dark winter. Yet the false alarms and strident mandates inspire distrust in those of us who have learned to live with an ongoing sense of doubt.

Because at this point we still don't know, do we?

8

"I'm going to lose the script," said the director of the Centers for Disease Control, Dr. Rochelle Walensky, recently on national television, "and reflect on the feeling I have of impending doom. . . . Right now I'm scared," she confided, "as a wife, mother, and daughter."

"Wow," said the interviewer. "'Impending doom.' Can you explain?"

Even during the depths of the Depression or the turmoil of the Second World War, did any national leader ever utter such an ominous public statement? As a husband, father, and son, President Roosevelt most emphatically did not "lose the script" and say that the only thing we had to fear was "impending doom." This is the exact opposite of democratic leadership: an attempt to exert social control through fearmongering.

Obviously we're now in a race between the accelerating pace of public vaccinations and the multiplying variants of the coronavirus. Many European countries menaced with a fourth wave of infections are back in full lockdown. Just as England was shut down for Christmas, France cleared the streets for Easter. Effectively, what Walensky is trying to do with her warning of "impending doom" is to cancel spring.

And the young, both here as well as in Europe, want no part of it. In Brussels, thousands of young Wallons, or francophone Belgians (among my ancestral people), were blasted by police water cannons as they stormed through the nocturnal streets demanding more social liberties. Maybe like my great-great grandfather Glaudot, some might immigrate to New Orleans, where the bars are now open until 11:00 p.m. And although we no longer speak French, *mes cousins*, I can promise that here you'll never hear a word of Flemish.

In this country, where a majority of us older alley cats have gotten our shots, infections are now spiking among those thirty-nine years of age or younger. Yet at that age, at which many feel immortal, I doubt that the doomsday prophecies of the director of the CDC will strike the fear of the Lord into them. In counterpoint to "impending doom," another phrase we're beginning to hear to animate the vaccination drive is "the light at the end of the tunnel." Like the chorus of cant about "flattening the curve" with which we were bombarded a year ago, the more these words are repeated, the less they mean, until we tune out the background noise of the pandemic.

Yet in the midst of this cacophonous din about "impending doom" and "a light at the end of the tunnel," restrictive decisions are still being made that, as if springing out of nowhere, can upend our lives. This weekend I attended the funeral of a lifelong friend, Lee Meitzen Grue, an eighty-seven-year-old poet and writer who I met during the seventies. Along with every other stray cat, dog, musician, and poet who crossed her path, she adopted me, and when passing through New Orleans I stayed with her, becoming part of her family. Or she visited me several times, both in Spain and San Francisco. Lee and her riverboat-pilot husband, Reggie, revealed something to me that I never expected: that my native city, scenario of a dark, claustrophobic childhood, could be fun. And that as an eccentric native son, there was a place for me here, where eccentricity is cultivated as a personality trait.

She lured me home, even finding me the teaching position at Tulane that brought me home from Barcelona in 1996.

At the funeral, I was looking forward to seeing not only her now ex-husband and her two sons, but particularly her daughter, Celeste, confined to a wheelchair with late-term multiple sclerosis. Celeste, as vitally creative as her mother, had married Tony Delafose, a Creole zydeco musician, and they settled in Lafayette, where they had raised two sons. As her condition worsened and bad luck would have it, she was admitted to a Catholic nursing home, the Château de Notre Dame, in New Orleans two days before the pandemic lockdown, and hadn't been permitted to visit face-to-face with any family or friends during the past year. But now those restrictions had been lifted, and I was assured that her husband had secured a suitable van, a wheelchair, and permission for her to attend her mother's funeral. Celeste had even received the second dose of the Pfizer vaccine in preparation for her fleeting reentry into the world, an hour-long visit to the mortuary to bid her mother goodbye.

But on the morning of the funeral and burial, she hadn't yet received a postive result on one of the highly unreliable post-vaccine antibody tests and was informed that if she left to attend the funeral she'd have to quarantine elsewhere for two weeks before she could return to the nursing home.

Even masked, I could tell that Tony was weeping, even as their two stalwart sons sat upright in the pews reserved for only twenty-five family members and close friends. (The mortuary originally cited eight as the limit, but the restrictions had broadened with newer guidelines). Everyone had been vaccinated, everyone wore face masks, we kept our distance, but Celeste was not allowed to attend her mother's farewell.

The absence of this dying woman in a wheelchair was louder than her presence as I stepped up to gather Tony into an embrace. "*C'est vraimanet cruel*," we consoled each other in Creole, "*la plus triste de tout*." Celeste hadn't seen her mother in more than a year, and she herself would not be long with us.

Later at the repast, as we sipped wine and ate bread pudding on Lee's porch, I noticed the elaborate wheelchair lift that the mother had constructed so that her crippled daughter could come to visit. Lee herself had wound up using it in the final months of her life.

Thank you, Dr. Walensky, but these often-arbitrary public health restrictions have overshadowed your "ominous doom" on a heartbreaking daily level with which your statistics, data, and science can never compete. That same week I learned that a good friend's husband, suffering from the dementia of Parkinson's disease, had been kicked out of the memory unit of Poydras Home, an expensive private nursing facility, because the directors had decided to remodel it. Just as he'd finally settled into a familiar bed and a daily routine among a few recognizable faces, some administrator had the bright idea to get rid of those blank-faced geezers to redesign the floor plan and color scheme. As in the case of Celeste, I can't imagine a more heartless decision.

I've come to distrust corporate health administrators even more than public health bureaucrats. Healthcare consumes 17.7 percent of our gross domestic product, grows faster than inflation every year, and employs 12 percent of the workforce, yet in both the spheres of public and private medicine, profits and prestige seem to count for more than the personal lives of patients. And for all of our financial investment, the United States has one of the worst health systems in the industrialized world.

Under a darkened sky it rained continuously that day during the afternoon memorial, as it had all week, while we read poems for Lee Grue, feeling not only the absence of our deceased friend but of a daughter mourning her mother from a nursing home bed she was forbidden to leave.

It was a dark, soggy tunnel of a memorial, and even squinting, I couldn't see the light at the end of it.

9

It was decades ago in Kovalam, India, a small beach town in the southeastern state of Kerala, where I first heard about vaccine hesitancy or regret. Before heading to India late in the winter of 1977, Greek friends in Athens, with whom I was visiting at the time, insisted that I go to the Department of Public Health to be vaccinated against such tropical diseases as typhoid. And there I was advised to take quinine pills to help ward off malaria, for which there was no vaccine.

In Kovalam, where my girlfriend Maureen and I were renting a cottage, the sole source of fresh drinking water was a well, where women in saris would line up with plastic buckets to fill. Although drawing water was considered a woman's task, as a foreign man dressed in a batik lungi, I was also allowed to wait among them, at first sparking a few shy titters and giggles. I would speak with the few women who knew some English and once asked one how many children she had, which I knew would be a source of pride.

"Only two," she answered with downcast eyes.

"I'm sure such a strong and lovely mother will have more," I said.

"I can't." Her eyes darted away from mine, as if embarrassed to reveal such intimate details to a foreign man. "Two years ago the Americans gave me a transistor radio to get sterilized."

I was dumbfounded. "That can't be true," I muttered. Perhaps India did need some form of population control, but I couldn't believe that Americans of any persuasion had gone about bribing women with transistor radios to become sterilized.

"And the radio no good anymore!" She raised her fierce glare to meet this American's. "Only one station work."

This was disturbing information, so I questioned a few of the more educated villagers in Kovalam. A schoolteacher told me that two years ago, an American medical team had been there to vaccinate the people against the smallpox epidemic. And yes, they did indeed offer transistor radios to many who agreed to be inoculated.

"But the woman at the well told me it made her sterile," I said.

"Rubbish," the schoolteacher said, a hint of impatience in his clipped British accent. "Somebody noticed that one of the vaccine bottles had the word 'sterile' on its label and spread this nonsense. I can assure you that many of those women have had babies after they were vaccinated, and nobody has fallen ill with smallpox ever since."

This was in 1978, and two years earlier the World Health Organization had mounted a massive campaign in the more remote parts of rural India to eradicate smallpox. On May 8, 1980, the W.H.O. declared the complete eradication of smallpox in the world, the greatest achievement of international public health. At this point I suspect that woman at the well is the mother of half a dozen more children and grandmother of half the village of Kovalam, mesmerized by Bollywood movies on her iPhone.

Yet deeply ingrained folk beliefs change slowly. As it did with the smallpox vaccine, in the near the future the W.H.O. will have to mount another herculean campaign to immunize the entire Indian subcontinent against the coronavirus, where the highly contagious Delta variant has already killed a reported 400,000 people, although the actual number of mortalities is suspected to be more than four million. This lethal variation is spreading like a wildfire, now accounting for 83 percent of the infections in the United States and even more alarming percentages in Europe and the Middle East. The Delta mutation is responsible for most of the recently hospitalized patients here in Louisiana. In India, where vaccines are hard to come by, only a fraction of the population has been inoculated, even though, ironically, Indian laboratories manufacture most brands of the other vaccines distributed throughout the world. And the W.H.O. will probably need another supply of electronic gadgets to tempt villagers. Vaccine hesitancy may account for this low rate, especially in rural India, where many believe that smearing themselves with the dung of the sacred cow, or drinking its urine, will protect them from the current pandemic. After elaborate yogic ceremonies, the dried cow dung is then washed off in ritual baptisms of milk.

The woman at the well represented my first experience with vaccine hesitancy, and as unfamiliar with the concept as I was, I witnessed forty years ago how these myths first get started. For those of us growing up during the fifties and sixties in the United States, there was a blithe assurance about receiving the smallpox vaccine, although we had no concept of the disfiguring pustules with which the highly contagious pox presented. In order to continue in school, our parents marched us down to the local school board, or a traveling nurse visited our classrooms, where we rolled up our sleeves to expose the upper left arm. The shot left a dime-sized dent that swelled into an itchy bump, blistering into a permanent scar. Horsing around, we sometimes compared our moon-shaped scars because each was unique, yet it would have been a shock at the public pool to come across another kid without one. Although by now disappeared, I carried my smallpox battle scar for years. These slowly fading public health stigmata served as the first vaccination passports, required among students, employees, and especially regional transplants, immigrants, or as we say in Louisiana, "people from away."

In those days, it was inconceivable to bribe people to be vaccinated, as it is today. Rather than transistor radios, now people in New

Orleans are being offered free po'boys, beignets, crawfish, or beers when they choose to be vaccinated against the coronavirus. One site with live music stages, food booths, and medical tents styled itself as Vax Fest, or a Jazz Fest with syringes, and the state has just set up the Shot-at-a-Million-Dollar lottery registration for the inoculated.

Yet still the Louisiana vaccination rate hovers below 40 percent, one of the lowest in the nation. We're told the hesitancy has something to do with urban or rural, red or blue, religion or politics, race or age. Many younger people, like the woman at the well in Kerala, fear infertility.

Last week my niece and her husband, on route from Lodi, California, to her native Lafayette, briefly passed through New Orleans to introduce me to my first grandniece, an eighteen-month-old girl. The month before I'd asked my niece on the phone if she was vaccinated and she said no, insisting that she planned to have more children. She has a master's degree, is a bilingual social worker and, although raised strictly Catholic in Cajun country, is now an evangelical Christian. I'm not sure how she resolves the exacting science called for in her social work with her dogmatic faith.

Exasperated, I was about to tell her the story about the woman at the well in India with her American transistor radio, but decided not to. It was just as well, because by the time the family arrived in New Orleans, she was recently pregnant with a second child, so we celebrated that.

I understand her concerns, but doubt that she or anyone else in her family will ever be vaccinated in the rural town where they live in northern California. And to try to reason with her would be as if I had chased after the woman at the well in Kovalam, insisting that she wasn't infertile because the vaccine label used the word "sterile," and now she'd never get smallpox, could have many more children, and get that cheap transistor radio fixed.

The eradication of the smallpox plague was one of the major triumphs of global public health, and this vaccine represented a centuries-long effort to wipe out a hideous killer. The first attempt was pioneered in the Americas in 1721, when none other than the Puritan preacher Cotton Mather learned from a West African slave about "variolation," or the practice of incising the skin with a shard of glass containing pustules of smallpox fluid. Yet since these first primitive inoculations, much more sophisticated vaccines have failed in the past, such as the defective first batch of the Salk polio vaccine in 1954, one that I was lucky enough to have received in a more successful form a year later. Public health has to do a better job of explaining what those "sterile" vials of serum contain and why they want to stick needles in people's arms. Charts, graphs, and statistics seldom magnetize the masses.

I wish that free transistor radios and po'boys could lure the multitudes to the mountaintop to rid the world of pestilence, but often science, like religion, is also a matter of faith.

And as with communion, baptisms, bar mitzvahs, or any other spiritual ritual, sometimes you just have to roll up your sleeve and do it.

10

Consider this invitation: "Fly the friendly skies to a long-postponed celebration at a fabulous destination where you could easily sicken and die."

This summer to date, twenty-six athletes have tested positive for the coronavirus and are quarantined in their quarters, eliminated from competing in their sports. Most of the world is wondering why the 2020 Olympic Games, postponed for a year, are being held in Tokyo in the first place, since the stadiums are emptied of a viewing public. At the spectacular fireworks that kicked off these summer games, many more Japanese were outside protesting the event than the few dignitaries allowed to be seated inside. One protestor thrust a sign into the TV camera that read "Don't Come to Japan." The whole country is in a state of emergency, with only 19 percent of the population vaccinated, while in Tokyo alone almost three thousand new cases occur every day.

Can such a loudly heralded anomaly really be happening even as the W.H.O. reports a fourth surge of worldwide infections by means of the highly transmissible Delta variant?

Few understand the high-stakes economics and politics at Olympic sites, which steamroll through a city years in advance, displacing everything in their way like an occupying army. In the autumn of 1991, while walking down Las Ramblas in Barcelona, I was already commenting to disbelieving local friends that "within a year, all these traditional old businesses will be T-shirt shops blaring flamenco pop and selling souvenir Spanish fans made in China." I was pointing at the ornate lettering of the signs above family-run tobacconists, pharmacies, and tailors. "It will all be tourist schlock. I've seen it happen in my native city after the 1984 World's Fair in New Orleans."

The Catalan national bird, I joked in a bad bilingual pun, was now the *grua*—that is, the industrial crane, not the long-legged waterfowl—those whirling beaked machines that loomed over every horizon while digging up the city. Even as a decently paid university professor at the Autonomous University, I couldn't find an affordable apartment in the center of the city, and so moved a commutable distance to the seaside town of Sitges. There, as I've mentioned, I was pitched into my own crisis moment during the AIDS epidemic.

Now Barcelona's center is worse than I could have imagined before the 1992 Olympics. The funky, old industrial port is filled with a stretch of sand masquerading as a glamorous faux beach, and the former hub of civic culture, Las Ramblas, is mobbed with Germans and Brits in bikinis and flip-flops. The Olympic Games unleashed in Barcelona what is now called el *turismo barato y borrracho*: cheap, drunk tourism. During the Olympic prelude, international financiers invested millions, then after the games flew the coop with billions, while locals lost the very shirts on their backs as traditional businesses developed over many generations were reduced to a single formula for survival: serving bad sangria to foreign conventioneers wearing lanyards.

This much I understand: the worldwide pandemic may have postponed the Olympics for a year but couldn't halt the express train of greed in Tokyo once it roared out of the station. More than 15.4 billion dollars were spent to stage these Olympic Games—the most expensive summer Olympics ever—inside of empty new stadiums. Meanwhile thousands of new infections are reported daily in Tokyo and the Japanese are urged to stay at home in semi-lockdown, with the sale of alcohol prohibited in restaurants that are supposed to close at eight in the evening, although these mandates are largely ignored.

On the local front, during what is being called this fourth surge of the pandemic, the mayor of New Orleans has just issued a mask "advisory," which means you should wear a face mask but don't have to. And among locals and tourists, few do. Yet New Orleans & Company, the city's destination branding agency, and the Convention Center are investing two million dollars in an ad campaign to lure conventioneers back to the city. At the same time, Louisiana has one of the lowest vaccination rates in the country and leads all of the other states in new infections. And speaking of drunken tourism, the 2020 Jazz Fest and French Quarter Festival events, both initially postponed like the Olympics, have been rescheduled for three consecutive weekends in October, two months from now. And if that isn't enough to lure the tipsy masses to cavort, add to this lineup a midweek concert by the Rolling Stones, postponed two years ago because of Mick Jagger's heart surgery.

Please allow me to introduce myself, a man of wealth and fame. And what's troubling you is the nature of my game.

I feel little sympathy for those devils at the opposite ends of the cultural spectrum, in restrained Japan as well as in wild-ass Louisiana, among the least vaccinated and most infectious populations on earth. Both are caught up in a tizzy of neurotic impulses stuck on stupid between medical and financial considerations. They're inviting us to long-postponed events to finally cash in on plans made long before the first coronavirus patient was ever put on a hospital respirator. The revenge of the postponed is similar to what Freud called the revenge of the repressed: there's much to be feared when the long-avoided finally rears its ugly head.

So come on over, y'all, and get down. Athletes, musicians, event administrators, and flimflam financiers have to eat too, no matter what it costs the rest of us.

11

We thought it would over by now.

We'd already put away our masks and made plans to continue our lives with classes, travel, concerts, and festivals. Real life seemed so long ago, and we were ready to get back to it. Yet as Dr. Atul

Gawande observes today, "people are almost angry about the reality of where we are now."

Over the past week, 24,147 cornonavirus patients have been hospitalized in Louisiana, at a daily average of more than two thousand cases a day. This current surge began a month ago and represents an increase of 150 percent, with almost six hundred recent deaths reported. This fourth wave of Delta variant infections is expected to crest by next month, mid-September of 2021. Most of the postponed festivals and concerts scheduled to resume this October in New Orleans have just been canceled, including Jazz Fest for the second year in a row, the Rolling Stones, and the Red Dress Run, a marathon of drunken men stumbling along in red frocks. At the last minute, White Linen Night, the annual festive art walk in the Warehouse District planned for this Saturday, has been also been called off. After gearing up all summer for a profitable autumn, the tourism industry has once again taken a bruising nosedive.

And more restrictions, they tell us, are on the way.

Emotions are running high, especially here in Louisiana, at the top of the list in the United States for new cases and at rock-bottom for the percentage of vaccinations. Yesterday it seemed as if I vexed a good friend, a sports fan who was rooting for our home team of the vaccinated against those challenging bastards, the unvaccinated. Of course, I share her sound reasoning, although not her grandstanding of those twin emotions now so prevalent everywhere: fear and anger. Perhaps because I've never been a team sports follower, much less a military man, I have a hard time viewing this pandemic as a game between competing good guys and bad guys, one that can be won or lost, or a battlefield in which some final victory can be claimed to the triumphant blare of trumpets.

"I think we'll be living with this mess this for the rest of our lives," I told my fellow septuagenarian, to an audible groan. "So we'd better get used to it. While we're fighting the Delta variant from India, a country where more than four hundred thousand have died, the Epsilon mutation is probably brewing in Peru, or the Zeta in Nigeria. If 90 percent of the population here was to be vaccinated, and our borders sealed for the next five years, then perhaps we Americans could see an end to it. But otherwise, these plagues go on for decades, if not centuries, disappearing and then reappearing in various new incarnations."

"Thank you for that uplifting thought," she said, abruptly ending the conversation.

I was eerily prescient in naming Peru as the source of the next variant to menace us, although wrong about the Greek letter attached to it. In an interview published today in the *New Yorker*, Dr. Gawande speaks of the Lambda mutation that has exploded in Peru, of which the first cases turned up in Houston last week. And he agrees with my grim prediction that the pandemic might prove to become endemic during our lifetimes:

> Is our goal to eliminate the virus entirely from our shores? And unless we get vaccination at exceedingly high levels, not just in the United States, but across the entire world, that's not going to happen. There are too many reservoirs for infection to come back in. Becoming endemic means that we may have circulation of virus in pockets, especially unvaccinated pockets that continues for awhile, and may continue for the foreseeable future.

Contagious endemic diseases, which recur in waves according to seasons and personal behavior, are common everywhere: tuberculosis, hepatitis, syphilis, gonorrhea, influenza, bacillary dysentery, pneumonia, measles, and mumps. Historically, most were once lethal pandemics, but we gradually learned how to treat and survive them.

Smallpox is the only disease ever to be completely eradicated through mass vaccinations, along with polio, which has almost disappeared. On the other hand, we know we can't eliminate these other ongoing endemic infections with shutdowns, health mandates, or crowd control. Except in China, we've learned not to spit in public to avoid tuberculosis, and how to use condoms to avoid sexually transmitted diseases. Kids with the measles or mumps are kept home from school. There are annual flu shots and nationwide bacterial food inspections. Endemic means a disease that will be among us for a long time and with which we've learned how to cope.

Yet people now find the idea of an endemic coronavirus pandemic hard to accept, especially those team-players like my friend who have done everything right: quarantined during the initial lockdown, been vaccinated, worn a face mask, socially distanced, and washed their hands. We're the good guys, they insist, on the right team that has practiced all of the perfect plays.

So why is our team losing?

To answer that question, I've been leafing through the famous diary of the seventeenth-century English naval administrator Samuel Pepys, one who punctiliously documents not only the bubonic plague outbreak in London in 1665, but the great fire that destroyed the city years later. The plague surged through mid-millennial London during several extended periods: in 1592, 1603, 1625, and 1636, as well as in the years that Pepys observes it, 1665 and 1666. This is the same epidemic episode that Daniel Defoe evokes in the thinly fictionalized *A Journal of the Plague Year*, written several decades later in 1721, when plague again threatened the city. Defoe is the more imaginative writer, but Pepys's day-to-day accounts lend perspective in detailed parallels to the rollercoaster ride that we've been going through with the coronavirus.

For instance, he comments on the various closings, openings, and resumed closings of public places. On New Year's Eve of 1665, he's in a celebratory mood and writes that "to our great joy, the town fills apace, and shops begin to open again. Pray God continue the plague's decrease—for that keeps the Court away from the place of business, and all goes to wrack as to public matters." That is exactly how we felt this June, before the Delta variant surge erupted at the end of July. Shops were opening, people getting back to business, and public matters being resumed.

Yet on April 5, 1665, only four months later, he writes of another surge that threatens the stability of the country, much like the one we're experiencing now: "The plague is, to our great grief, increased nine this week, though decreased a few in the total. And this increase runs through many parishes, which makes us fear for next year." At this point he notices the proliferation of red crosses hanging on the front doors of those neighbors who have died in the epidemic, markers inscribed with the prayer: "Lord have mercy on our souls."

And thus it goes, back and forth, from the optimistic reopening to the despair of reclosing public spaces, until he fears a general breakdown of the state. On October 1, 1665, he writes: "Things here must break in pieces, every man his own business of profit or pleasure; and that certainly the kingdom could not stand this condition long—which I fear."

The prudent Mr. Pepys does the best he can to survive: he chews tobacco to ward off the contagion and, when traveling throughout England, lies that he isn't from plague-ridden London but rather rural Woolwich, where he has installed his wife and children. This, of course, calls to mind how wealthy New Yorkers retreated from the pandemic that first hit their city in the spring of last year and headed for their country homes. Pepys also mentions a conspiracy theory worthy of a Facebook post: he no longer wears his fashionable wigs, because the hair in these gentlemanly headpieces is rumored to be taken from the corpses of plague victims.

Finally, on November 20, 1666, eighteen months after the plague first erupted during this outbreak in London, church bells are rung to announce the end of the epidemic. But Pepys wonders if this is too premature and whether another surge might soon afflict the city: "Thence to church, it being thanksgiving-day for the cessation of the plague; but, Lord! They say that it is hastened before the plague is quite over, there dying some people still."

The outbreak that Pepys chronicles in 1665–66 killed approximately a fourth of London's population at the time—100,000 out of 460,000 residents—yet by no means was the most lethal of the many instances in which bubonic plague infected various cities throughout history. Although traces of the bubonic plague have been discovered in Bronze Age skeletons, the first recorded outbreak in the West occurred in Pelusium, Egypt, in 541 AD, and during the ongoing centuries its recurring variants ravaged medieval Europe, killing one-third to one-half of the population.

Now we're able to treat the disease, even though it seldom occurs. Actually, several years ago, a friend's husband contracted bubonic plague here in New Orleans. While working along the Mississippi River around a grain elevator swarming with rats, he evidently was bitten by one of their fleas, sickened, and diagnosed with bubonic plague. Millennia since its initial appearance in the Western world, we finally have a cure for it. The patient was given a shot of antibiotics, then went home to barbecue spare ribs. After two thousand years, trials are currently underway for a vaccine to prevent the bubonic plague, based on the COVID-19 model.

Now that is what I'd call progress—slow, painstaking, and methodical as it has proven to be throughout the centuries. I wish that we were in such a final inning of our protracted match against the coronavirus, but at this point I doubt that we've even finished the first game of the series. The pandemic has brought out of the best of our civic team spirit, especially among healthcare workers, along with the worst in human nature. Yet I'm afraid that the opposing side isn't other citizens, no matter how wrongheaded their decisions may prove to be, but a wily virus that may temporarily conquer the world with its devious variants.

Frankly, I suspect that we older Americans needn't reserve our ringside seats, because we won't be around to cheer the brass bands on their victory march when the disease is finally defeated.

While we slug it out with the Delta variant, the Peruvian Lambda and perhaps next the Nigerian Zeta have yet to enter the stadium, and who knows what surprise tactics those mutations may bring to the game. Mid-epidemic, on May 24, 1665, Pepys wrote that "the news is of the plague growing upon us in this towne; and of remedies against it: some saying one thing, some another."

"What does history teach?" asked Gertrude Stein. "History teaches."

12

Today my niece tells me that through her church she's ordered a study guide to the Book of Revelations, the final gospel of the New Testament. After all, she lives in Lodi, forty miles from the Caldor wildfire, one of the many raging out of control in northern California and elsewhere around the world this summer. The air in Lodi is so smoky that she can't let her antsy twenty-month-old go outside to play and, although due to give birth to a second child in January, is still undecided about the getting the vaccine, risking an infection for all three at once. She's convinced this must be the apocalypse, especially while watching the coverage of the violence at the Kabul airport during the chaotic evacuation of Americans and their supporters after this country's twenty-year debacle in Afghanistan.

Scraggly Taliban beards and primeval coronavirus spikes: what a menacing combination. Throughout the ages, war and plague have always been paired in the same phrase. The Four Horsemen of the Apocalypse first galloped through the Book of Revelations, in which pestilence rides a white horse, war a red one, famine a black one, and death itself a pale one. These ghastly riders "were given authority . . . to kill with sword, famine, plague, and by any means the beasts of the earth" (Revelations: 6:7–8). The Spanish flu pandemic became globally virulent in the trenches of World War I, and the worst of the polio epidemic erupted in the United States following World War II.

During this past year, the coronavirus pandemic, widespread hunger, mass shootings, and internal wars have emerged simultaneously, one seemingly from the other. Hospital wards packed with COVID-19 patients, public food pantries, crazed violence, climatic disasters, and tribal tensions have dominated our attention as much as John of Patmos ever could have imagined, writing Revelations alone in the desert two millennia ago.

During the darkest days of this pandemic, senselessly violent conflicts have erupted all over the earth, most notably in Myanmar, Israel, Cuba, and Ethiopia. These bloody encounters, some approaching civil wars, mirror this past summer's riots provoked by racial protests in the United States, along with the attempted coup d'état of January 6.

Once again, fear and anger are twin sides of the same coin. And when angry, who better to take it out on than those who most resemble you, your compatriots but of a different stripe or hue: Israelis vs. Palestinians, Buddhist vs. Muslim Burmese, redneck cops vs. poor Blacks, red- state Americans vs. blue-state ones? The ongoing death and destruction of pestilence must be the fault of *those other people*: our own kin but marked by some sectarian difference. Freud blamed this type of internecine fratricide on what he called an exaggerated "degree of narcissism": a hatred for those neighbors just like us except for a single degree of difference.

We continue to live at the corner of Cain and Abel Streets, and much like the aging Mark Twain, late in life I've grown cynical about human nature. The flower child in me, who headed west to San Francisco more than half a century ago to "let the sunshine in" and create a more peaceful and loving world, is now a wreath of desiccated daisies. Perhaps it has taken this pandemic to punctuate my own profound distrust about who we are as a species, a recently evolved one but with deep genetic roots in our murderous prehuman ancestors.

Only 7 percent of our DNA is unique to the relatively modern dominance of contemporary humans, the rest inherited from now-extinct Neanderthals and Denisovans, who were in turn descended from bands of killer apes. This may explain why, at the moment, human nature strikes me as an open sewer, and reeling from the stench, I realize how much I've come to value manhole covers. Religion, the arts, education, law, science, and language, those manhole covers developed throughout the past few millennia—that is, everything we call civilization—are there for a reason, to keep what Christians call "original sin" from rising to engulf us. And throughout history, as every commentator on plagues has emphasized, pandemics seem to pry loose these cloacal covers to show us what really lies beneath.

And so it is during pestilence, as civilization breaks down, wars erupt, and tribal hatreds surface, that we stick our heads back into these foul waters. We don't need to visit distant Israel or Myanmar to witness this. Last month in Tennessee an anti-vaccination protestor drove her car through a tent of people waiting for their life-saving shots. At the same time, a railway worker in San Jose, on a Bay Area train line I know only too well, murdered nine of his coworkers in a mass shooting, claiming to be fed up with his colleagues. And he wasn't alone. During the first five months of 2021, there have been 232 mass shootings in this country, almost two a day, and it's difficult to discern which Horseman of the Apocalypse is responsible. Has the viral war inside our own bodies provoked another one against each other?

In Sunday school I was taught that we mortals need to be "saved." Frankly, I always wondered: saved from what?

Now I know: saved from ourselves.

In a sense, the need for the manhole covers of civilization to contain the sewer of humanity at its worst mirrors the heated debate both here and in Europe about the necessity for gatekeepers in social media, boiling over with every stripe of uncensored vileness, vanity, and divisive groupthink the human brain can conceive. In a recent article in the *New Yorker* ("Facebook's Broken Vows"), Jill Lepore blames unregulated social media for "a loneliness epidemic, the growth of political extremism and political violence, the widening of political polarizations, the decline of democracy, a catastrophic crisis in journalism, and an unprecedented rise in propaganda, fake news, and misinformation." Friends are often curious about why I choose not to participate in these feral digital platforms rife with bullying, gossip, semiliterate thought-farts, conspiracy theories, and photo-shopped selfies.

I know what's down there but simply don't want to smell or swim in it.

It stands to reason that the four countries in which the coronavirus has blazed out of control have been those led by populist nationalists seething with separatist vitriol, all great manipulators of social media: Jair Bolsonaro in Brazil, Narendra Modi in India, Boris Johnson in the United Kingdom, and, of course, Donald Trump in the United States. That is, Bolsonaro, with his racist, homophobic rhetoric, Modi with his anti-Islamic venom, Johnson, architect of the anti-European Brexit, and Trump, who wanted to make America great again by isolating us from those "shithole countries" in the rest of the world.

Now that we've gained some modicum of optimistic perspective with the heroic vaccination efforts, it's time to put the manhole covers of civilization back in place. Soon, we hope, students will return to in-person classes, congregations will reassemble in churches and temples, and, currently in danger of being distanced to death in the virtual world, culture will again blossom with in-person concerts, cinemas, book events, exhibitions, lectures, conferences, theater performances, and public celebrations. And we can lower our masks, regard each once again other at a close distance with mutual trust, and smile.

Or will the wily virus win? Not necessarily the rapidly mutating coronavirus with which we're now struggling, but that ancestral contagion that threatens us when the four biblical horsemen of pestilence, war, famine, and the vengeful natural world gallop toward us all at once over the horizon.

13

To date, the cornavirus has killed one out of every five hundred Americans, and as the Delta variant surge continues to peak, on a late August afternoon I once again catch myself asking that fateful question, the turning point in every tragic plotline: "What else can go wrong?"

And suddenly, on the last weekend of this month, the horseman galloping toward me isn't riding the white horse of pestilence but is mounted on another apocalyptic steed, one that represents the vengeful natural world as recounted in the Old Testament, with its locust plagues, searing droughts, and planetary floods. But I can't make out this horse's particular color because the lights have gone out.

Along with the air-conditioning, phone, and internet. On August 29, the monster storm Katrina celebrates her sweet sixteenth birthday, inviting along her kid sister Ida, a hurricane even stronger and more devastating than the destructive bitch of the older sibling storm that changed New Orleans forever in 2005.

Like clockwork, Hurricane Ida arrives late on Sunday evening, on the same date as her big sister, but stays twice as long, all day Monday. I confess that I love hurricanes since I was born during one, and so literally sleep like a baby through much of this one, as if rocked in a cradle on a wind-tossed sea. I finally wake to the tail end of a message blaring from my answering machine. As I race to the landline phone, a friend's voice is warning

". . . and they say the power may be out for two weeks or more."

At that very moment, the power goes out.

I grew up here and know the hurricane drill: my cell phone is charged, flashlights and candles at hand, a portable radio loaded with fresh batteries, the refrigerator stocked with food along with jugs of frozen water to keep the insides chilled as long as possible, bottles of wine line the kitchen counter, and the bathtub is filled with water to flush the toilet in case the waterline is cut off. Yet still, I was hoping against hope that this wouldn't happen—not again, not now—after eighteen months of pandemic hysteria. Then the lights flicker back on.

Then off again.

They play with me for a few minutes before the power goes off. For good. And seemingly forever.

I snap from a drowsy dream state into manic action. Close the curtains to keep the cool air inside for as long as possible, then step outside into the hundred degree heat of the soupy air that I'll be living in for quite some time after I'm forced to open the windows.

The wind and rain are gusting outside, trees lashing back and forth, the sky swirling, the heavens heaving down torrents of storm-water. This Marigny townhouse, constructed in 1859 three blocks from the Mississippi River, is on the highest land in the city, so there's no flooding. But I do notice that, oddly enough, it seems to be raining inside, sprinkling my stereo and turntable, which I cover with large plastic bags. I squint up at strips of paint dangling from the plaster of these twenty-one-foot ceilings. Nothing I can do now but turn on the cell phone and try to plot my immediate future. If I can get a signal, which I can't.

At the moment, little do I suspect that my immediate future will involve roasting in the dark, soggy basting pan of this apartment for the next four dog days of summer heat, trying to re-charge a cell phone from a neighbor's car idling in park, searching for a bag of ice to fill my ice chest, and dressed in little but boxer shorts, staring for endless hours into candlelight while listening to the classical music station on the battery-operated radio with headphones. As night falls, it's as if I'm at a séance that may never end, with visions of my Creole Glaudot ancestors reclaiming my sweat-drenched corpse as the pale rider, the fourth horseman of the apocalypse, reaches down to hoist me up onto his horse. We gallop toward the horizon until we join the white horse of pesti-lence, along with the red and black ones of war and famine, head-ing toward the airport in Kabul with spiked coronavirus spores emblazoned on our battle shields.

In case you haven't noticed, I'm delirious.

It's now Tuesday, August 31, 2021, and I wonder if those thousands of clamoring Afghani refugees managed to get out of the airport, or if the gurneys filled with COVID patients packing hospital hallways ever found places in the ICU. Those were the last images of the tumultuous outside world that I witnessed on my now-blank TV screen. Today feels like the deadline for something, if not the end of a senseless foreign war then maybe my own existence, as I sit waiting like a Beckett character in the dark inferno of a candlelit room for a pale rider—one named Godot, or perhaps my pépère Glaudot—to crack open the lid of this stifling barrel and pull me out.

I wait for four long nights, but he never comes.

14

The plan—and there's always a plan, even in the grimmest situations, isn't there?—is for my friends Marsha and Gary to drive down from Huntsville, Alabama, where Gary "blows up things for the government," as he likes to describe his current profession, and to evacuate me from this hellhole. Because the telecommunication satellite towers have fallen, I can't call anyone within my local area code unless they happen to be near a transmitter stationed far away from the Mississippi River, in which the city's cell phone reception towers now lay submerged. So my mobile 504 prefix number connects with Marsha's mobile 504 line only because she's in Huntsville, but wouldn't if she were here. It takes me a while to figure out these complexities. And, of course, I can easily reach Gary's San Francisco prefix of 415, former fellow flower child that he is. Hard as it is to imagine, I could call Madrid, but not my neighbor next door who has a locally prefixed cell phone.

Katrina was an engineering disaster, in which 80 percent of the city flooded after the poorly built federal levees breached, constructed at great expense by the Civil Corps of Engineers. In my own lifetime, that disaster occurred during an era before universal cell phone and internet dependence, and my landline continued to work. I simply ignored my dead cordless phone, plugged a Princess phone into a wall jack, and did an interview with the *New York Times*. Friends called me from San Francisco and Spain. During Ida the reconstructed levees in New Orleans have remained intact, but this storm has proven to be a technological disaster. Along with the power grid, our mobile phone and internet-driven lives have collapsed, leaving most of us dry but isolated and speechless inside our darkened homes. Nothing works, especially the complex web of technology on which we've become so dependent. With most of the cell phone towers in the city offline, and all digital communication paralyzed, we feel like mute amputees. How vulnerable—and open to some stealthy but bloodless foreign drone attack—our electronic lives have made us. Take out a dozen major urban satellite towers in the United States, and without firing a shot, the entire country would collapse into the chaos in which I'm now living.

One problem with my friends' evacuation plan is that since there's no electricity, the fuel pumps aren't working, so there wouldn't be any gasoline for the drive back. And the lines for those few pumps operated by generators involve hour-long waits. In short, my friends' car could get them here but couldn't get us back out, because the energy outages are throughout the entire southeast part of the state.

What to do? I sweat, they ponder, and we talk and wait.

And four days later, the Thursday before my seventy-fourth birthday, a miracle occurs: the power pops back on in the French Quarter, where the electrical grid is underground. These friends maintain a *pied-à-terre* studio there on Royal Street, around the corner from the gallery apartment where I lived for twelve years on Dumaine Street. Actually, I was living there during Katrina, and in another star-crossed coincidence, my grandmother was born across the street. And this apartment's key is secured in a magnetic box attached to a washbasin in the courtyard.

A neighbor of theirs, one who I can reach because she has an out-of-town cell phone prefix, picks me up in her purple golf cart and helps me to drag the little food I've stored in a Styrofoam ice chest, along with a few belongings, to the Royal Street courtyard efficiency. After fiddling with the fuse box, the lights, air-conditioning, and ceiling fan miraculously pulse with life. So for me this catastrophe has become what some might imagine as a French Quarter getaway, complete with holiday digs in the heart of the festive City That Care Forgot. Except that all the storefronts are boarded up, and much like the pandemic lockdown, the only people in the streets are the more combative and less lucid of the homeless. As a matter of fact, these post-hurricane streets make the locked-down Quarter seem like a weekend party, with its clandestine clusters of COVID-defiant bad boys rattling the ice in their go-cups, masks dangling from one ear.

In this damp, shady courtyard, strewn with tree limbs downed by the hurricane, I feel right at home within this small community of artists and tattooed service workers, Quarter regulars of the kind I've known all my life. It could be 1968, when I had my first apartment in this neighborhood, but when I rush out to scrounge among the bare shelves of the only open grocery, now closing at 5 p.m., I'm reminded that it isn't.

I forget my face mask, required to enter.

The plague! How could I have forgotten about the pandemic that has been consuming us for the past eighteen months? Entering the store barefaced is as if, during the Nazi air raids over London during World War II, I'd entered an underground shelter with my fly unzipped. People stare, but no big deal. A tape of old Bob Dylan songs might be looping through my mind, but the stark realities that confront us now make those dark times of assassinations and civil rights demonstrations, Vietnam War resistance and bloody protest marches, seem like the good old days. At least then we were filled with naïve idealism, a yearning for changes that soon would make the world right and just.

Or so we'd hoped.

15

"Because for the past two years I've been miserable here, that's why," Harriette tells me on the phone.

I've been trying to reason with a close friend, my first love from high school, about why she's going to sell the house where she's lived in Atlanta for the past thirty-five years and move to Boise, Idaho, a place she's only visited briefly. Of course, her only child is now in Idaho, but this son and his wife are now packing up to move to Jackson Hole, a winter sports resort five hours away near Wyoming, where they'll be "working from home." They're in their early thirties, an age at which most of us roam. But Harriette has lived and worked for almost half a century in Atlanta, finishing a Ph.D., teaching, marrying twice in a city where almost all of her lifetime friends live.

"Idaho?" I ask. "For real? Look before you leap."

These days a lot of people are leaping before they look.

This stage of the seemingly endless pandemic is proving to be the Great Disruption in many people's lives. Economists are calling it the Great Resignation, claiming that just this past August almost four and a half million people in this country quit their jobs. During the same period in Louisiana, fifty-seven thousand resigned. Among Emergency Medical Service paramedics, many of the vacancies are due to burnout, and so hundreds of 911 calls for ambulances go unanswered every day. As of last month in New Orleans, there were twenty full-time vacancies out of 150 EMS positions.

But most people don't have jobs as stressful as paramedics or ICU nurses. Just as the pandemic seems to be waning, what's the reason for this massive uprooting? Everyone seems to be resigning, changing jobs, moving, dropping out of college or going back, dispersing, divorcing, pulling back from the few permanent connections they might have. The medical world appears to be in particular chaos. Both my cardiologist and primary care doctors are moving to new hospitals, and I can't keep track of their constantly shifting schedules. The longtime pharmacist at the French Quarter Walgreens has taken an early retirement, and now the pharmacy has cut back its hours and days of operation because of "staffing problems" with a rotating crew of subcontracted part-time pharmacists.

"Help Wanted" signs are posted on the doors of most neighborhood businesses. Many of those not "working from home" aren't working at all, and I don't understand how they can afford this after almost two years of lockdown joblessness. The additional federal supplement in monthly unemployment compensation payments (initially $2,400, and then $1,200) kept many families afloat, yet evidently left other people sitting pretty. A friend in another state, one with more generous unemployment benefits than Louisiana, claims to have socked away over forty thousand dollars on lockdown unemployment and now can afford to be choosey about when and where he returns to work, putting it off for as long as possible.

Everyone wants change, and they want it now. Tragically, even if that change means dying, as has too often been the case with spiking suicide and opioid overdose rates. Prolonged lockdown and social isolation have produced a suffocating feeling of stagnation. I can't imagine what will happen to those who have been told to permanently work from home and have moved to cheaper, more attractive locations. Eventually, as we might suspect, they will be replaced by algorithms, temp workers, or migrating millennials who will not only do the same job at half the salary but cheerfully bring back coffee and sandwiches for the office.

The secret of success at any job, I've always been told, is to make yourself indispensable. And how indispensable is any employee working for an IT company in Palo Alto while living in rural New Mexico, where the sunsets are more breathtaking but no backslapping water-cooler politics guarantee permanency or promotion?

Since couples have been cooped up together at home for the past eighteen months, you might expect the birth rate to be soaring. We call them storm babies in Louisiana, because when the power shuts off, as after a hurricane, what else do couples have to do in the dark? But during the pandemic the opposite has proven true. The birth rate has fallen, while divorces and domestic abuse cases are surging. People are lonely for social company, yet sick and tired of those with whom they've been caged up, easy targets for mounting anger. Teenagers are committing suicide in record numbers, condemned to the solitary confinement of scrolling through social media, and alcohol and tobacco sales have almost doubled. Obviously, when shut up at home, there are other ways to occupy your time besides making babies, such as drinking, smoking, and staring at digital screens.

A public health ad in the *New Yorker* warns that social isolation is as lethal as smoking fifteen cigarettes a day. I'm not sure how research data was tabulated for that unlikely comparison, but you get the point. The way in which we've been forced to live for the past eighteen months is lethal, saving our lives even if it kills us. And the number of friends I've lost during these past two years only rivals the peak of the AIDS epidemic.

Yet these friends didn't die of the coronavirus but of the harmful effects of isolation.

Frankly, rather than from isolation, I'd rather croak by chain-smoking fifteen cigarettes at an outdoor café, if I could find someone to accompany me.

The Kentucky writer Wendell Berry calls the post-World War II era the Great Disruption. That was when rural Americans migrated to cities, cars and freeways dispersed the intimacy of downtown neighborhoods with a vast displacement to the suburbs, televisions replaced front porch sitting as the communal evening activity, and people spoke through telephones, not over backyard fences while hanging laundry. Growing up in the fifties, I lived through the tail end of that social disruption and sympathize with Berry's nostalgia for what was lost.

As soon as my father bought his Studebaker, we moved away from those neighborhoods in downtown New Orleans bordering Esplanade Avenue, where our rental shotguns always were chosen to be within walking distance of family, schools, and churches. The car allowed us to strand ourselves in other neighborhoods filled with strangers. Watching TV instead of fanning ourselves in rocking chairs on front porches, we became strangers to each other. And, of course, during the infernal summer months, window air-conditioning units sealed the deal. We inhabited pods in which the only sounds were churning window units and the theme music from *Dragnet*.

And this was only the beginning, because, as we see now with other technological upheavals, our lives are changed bit by bit until we no longer remember who we are, used to be, or what alternatives exist. Car culture instigated the first stage of White Flight. In the midsixties, the automobile spurred my parents' inevitable move from the then integrating city to the all-White burbs. Which was when I dropped out and moved back in with my grandparents in Mid-City during high school. The alienating displacement of car-and-TV pod life wasn't for me. I preferred to catch the streetcar down to the French Quarter, which during that era was a grimy port neighborhood run by the Mafia and peopled by pimps, prostitutes, and sailors, not to mention the main attraction for me: artists, writers, musicians, and civil rights activists.

The post-World War II era accelerated these long-brewing changes in American life, just as the pandemic has speeded up a

Second Great Disruption, the electronic world in which we're now living. Like weightless astronauts in digital space, we've abandoned our own bodies, whether our skin tone is black, brown, or white. Online, we're all neutered and homogenized, with no accents, body odors, or eye colors. Yet we're often surprised when confronted face-to-face with other Americans who look, sound, and smell different from ourselves.

The virtual life is the final stage of White Flight.

"This feels like World War III," somebody blurted out to me last month, in shock at some new discombobulating facet of a pandemic that has left five million people dead around the world. Yet this fall, even as the pandemic deaths appear to be dwindling in the United States, the real disruptions to our lives have lingered in a more pernicious permanence. After pestilence, as after wars, we wake from nightmares determined to create new lives. Yet these new lives, like Wendell Berry's portrait of the nascent emptiness of fifties stripmall America, can never be foreseen or erased. We never look before we leap, as world tragedies push us toward the cliff edges of the endurable.

And so as we fall, we hope change is on the way, if only *that thing* that has oppressed us for so long would go away.

Stagnating in place at the moment, what has my own change fantasy been like? As an inveterate world traveler who now dreads airports, it's dreaming. Delicious fantasies of sleep-induced roaming take me around the globe, to places I've lived or one day hoped to, in polyglot scenarios that take place in languages I speak fluently, or in those in which I can barely communicate, such as Mandarin Chinese, Catalan, Portuguese, or Italian. I'm renting a villa with some sexy guys in Rio, or dealing with stray ducks in my old apartment in the Barrio Gótico in Barcelona, complaining in Catalan to a cop, who tells me they escaped from a Swedish film set. I'm trying to buy a train ticket from Gerona to Lyon. Where am I headed, to meet a Spanish friend in Marseilles or Montpelier? Then on Halloween I'm walking up Telegraph Hill in San Francisco carrying a small ceramic skull. I'm speaking with the Beat poet Michael McClure, who has become a Lutheran choir director in Norway. Does he remember our old friends Philip Lamantia and Lawrence Ferlinghetti?

Every evening I can't wait to take off in the dreams that transport me around the world, no boarding pass required. And I hate to wake up, often lingering in bed hoping to return to Rio or Barcelona, Marseilles or San Francisco. My great escape has been to become a frequent-flier dreamer. I feel little need to act out the fantasies that obsess others around me, ones that will take them as far away from their unbearable lives as the strictly monitored borders of this pandemic will allow.

16

Boo.

Boo who?

It all depends on Boo, claims the New Orleans Health Department. Or rather, the data about coronavirus infections collected from Boo this month will determine whether we celebrate Carnival next year. The Krewe of Boo is a minor-league Halloween parade introduced a few years ago by Mr. Mardi Gras, Blaine Kern Jr., a prominent float builder, partly to keep the Carnival business abuzz during the autumnal lull and also to lure tourists to the city for Halloween. Much as in Mexico, another death-obsessed culture, Halloween is an elaborate spiritual holiday in the traditional way in which we locals celebrate it. This year the kitschy Krewe of Boo, disregarding tradition by a mile, rolled on a Saturday night a full week before All Hallows' Eve. At the last minute its route was cut short because of a severe police shortage, and few locals took the tacky parade seriously. A dozen mini-floats with spooky themes trailed behind an endless motorcade of important fat men waving at the crowd from methane-belching go-carts. Yet it was the city's first attempt at a street celebration in almost two years.

Among the viewers, more than half of whom were tourists, circulated nine masked staff members of the Public Health Department costumed as Dr. Fauci, in white lab coats and surgical scrubs. They were accompanied by thirty-nine data gals and guys in face masks carrying pumpkin-colored placards that read "Data Saves Lives (and Mardi Gras)." They went about collecting information from people in the crowd, such as their vaccination and COVID-testing status, as well as the contact cell phone links where they could be texted a medical questionnaire within two weeks. If a significant percentage of the contacts reported recent infections, Mardi Gras will be canceled, blaming it on—you know—Boo. If not, the carnival parade season would be scheduled for February of next year.

As it turns out that it has been.

This is the fun-filled way we do science in the City That Care Forgot. In addition to this random data from Boo, the Health Department is keeping an eye on the aftermaths of the Boston Marathon and the Macy Thanksgiving's Day Parade in New York, where no faux Faucis will circulate among the crowds.

On the evening of the actual holiday, I hosted a small costumed Halloween party at home here on Bourbon Street, where there are usually more tricks than treats, and then the next day went to St. Louis Cemetery Number Three for the Feast of All Saints, bringing white roses to the Glaudot tomb. Staring up from the steps of the tomb, I could spot only the cupola of the gloomy Luling Mansion next door, wondering how I could have lived in that haunted pile for five years. The vampire movie. The eviction. The sinister Kali *gris-gris* I left behind the mirror over the bedroom mantel to hex the landlord. Details of this past year came rushing back to me as I arranged white roses in a vase, memories that I suspected my plague-besieged Creole ancestors might understand. Their lives shared my own gothic plotlines.

An initial hotspot of infection, at this moment there are fewer patients hospitalized in New Orleans with the coronavirus than anywhere else in the United States or at any other time during the pandemic. Yet in spite of the upbeat jack-o-lanterns and white roses, I'm hesitating to celebrate this milestone too enthusiastically, trying to avoid the rollercoaster ride of gleeful victories and dismal relapses that Samuel Pepys recorded during the bubonic plague years in London.

Today, for the first time in the past eighteen months, the United States opened its borders to vaccinated airline passengers from thirty-nine previously blocked foreign countries, even though Germany, Austria, Holland, and Belgium are recording record surges in infections that threaten renewed lockdowns. Yet families and lovers are now free to reunite, and people from neighboring Mexico and Canada can enter by overland routes. Yet I can't help but ask what will these visitors, whether tourists or loved ones, bring with them? Now that the Delta mutation seems to have worn out its welcome here, which new foreign variant will spread like a forest fire among the 40 percent of unvaccinated Americans? Or if the new variant is vaccine-resistant, will it cause breakthrough infections among the vaccinated?

Once again, I return to the pivotal analogy of herd versus hive at the heart of contemporary epidemiology. Just as New Orleans residents are beginning to reach some degree of herd immunity among ourselves, are we ready to rejoin the global hive again? Will we go from a circle of bucks with raised horns protecting their herd from sick intruders back to the model of the global beehive, in which electronically connected insects buzz in and out in a one-for-all, all-for-one subservience to a digital queen?

This weekend I participate in my first public event in a long while: a monthly Saturday evening Art Walk among galleries on Julia Street in the Warehouse District. It's the inaugural night of this year's Prospect Art Project, dubbed Prospect 5. Both the art and the gallery-hoppers are much less edgy and avant-garde than I imagined and, though sparsely attended, much more cordial and relaxed. I go with my painter cousin to see a new exhibition of work by my friend Adrian Deckbar, one of whose paintings I chose for the cover of my recent collection of short stories, *You Don't Know Me*. I run across a few other friends and actually hug a couple.

Does this mean the pandemic is over?

Not really, because I'm mystified by the wildly inconsistent health protocols. Only one of the five galleries we visit asks for vaccination verification at the door, and as my cousin confides in me, that's because the owner fell ill at some point with the virus. Some people wear face masks inside the galleries, others don't. Some put them on at the door, then lower them to sip a cup of wine. Like my cousin, some are masked at one point, unmasked at others, for no discernible reason. A bizarre charade of peek-a-boo takes place: a masked person recognizes an unmasked friend, as happens to me several times, yet hardly ever the other way around. Then the masked people lower their face masks to talk, while out of courtesy the unmasked person fumbles to strap on theirs. All of this masking and unmasking is an arbitrary social performance, like the coy raising and lowering of lorgnette-style eye masks at a Venetian Carnival ball. Yet this isn't a flirtatious ritual that signals desire but a self-righteous one that signals virtue, a perverse ballet of public health that plays at appearing both cool and safe.

The beau of the ball, a featured ninety-four-year-old unmasked painter, hobbles along with a cane greeting everyone, while a twenty-year-old kid who just flew in from New York never takes her mask off as she glares from a corner. Which one has the most to fear from random infection, and what does the farcical protocol of face masks have to do with it?

The art is more precisely crafted than I'm used to seeing, as if artists have had more time to perfect their techniques during lockdown in their studios. I leave a bit tipsy on gallery wine, pleased that I've resumed a social activity that once felt so normal. Yet the ornate minuet of masking and unmasking, much like the data gatherers at the Halloween parade, is a nagging reminder that something is wrong. We're still nervous and on edge, waiting for some scary phantom to reappear at any moment from around a dark corner to grab normal life back from our tenuous grip.

Boo.

Got you.

17

Who could have seen it coming?

Indeed something has just grabbed us, in spite of the champagne bubble of local optimism generated by the Krewe of Boo and its faux Faucis. After Thanksgiving, a new coronavirus variant suddenly exploded out of South Africa just in time to make this Christmas as fraught and frightening as last year's. Much like what Samuel Pepys records in his diary about the rollercoaster ride of joyous remissions followed by devastating reappearances of the bubonic plague in seventeenth-century London: ladies and gentlemen, hang onto your hats and sanity.

This is going to be a bumpy ride.

Between the names of hurricanes and pandemic variants, we'll soon be as familiar with the Greek alphabet as Sophocles. Last summer the Gulf Coast was menaced by disastrous storms named (in alphabetical order) Delta, Epsilon, Zeta, Eta, and Iota. As of November of this past month, the fifth variant of the coronavirus, Delta, has replaced Alpha as the dominant world threat. Skipping various letters of the Greek alphabet—I'd have gone for a zinger like Zeta—this new strain christened as Omnicron is twice as transmissible with its fifty mutations. Just last month, the South African positivity test rate increased five-fold, and hospitalizations quadrupled.

Predictions are slippery about this wily virus. The Lambda variant from Peru that Dr. Atul Gawande warned us about this summer never took hold, in spite of a handful of infections in Texas. Just last month, the pandemic seemed to be stabilizing into an endemic disease, or so we thought. Sure, the 40 percent of unvaccinated Americans were still filling intensive care units, but vaccine mandate laws were being passed, more people were lining up for booster shots, and masks were coming off. Airplane flights were booked, Christmas turkeys stashed in freezers, Broadway theater marquees lit up, and concerts rehearsed.

Yet as winter temperatures plummeted, the Delta variant was still of major concern in many northern states, oddly enough in such vaccine-conscientious strongholds as Vermont and Rhode Island. In Maine and New York, the National Guard was called in to staff overwhelmed ICUs. As of earlier this fall, the Netherlands was again in full lockdown, and Austria, Belgium, Germany, France, and Ireland were passing more stringent quarantine laws, opposed by stormy youthful protest marches. Travelers from the United Kingdom, where the virus was surging unchecked, were banned from entering the European Union.

On the other hand, two antiviral medications were awaiting approval, the pills molnupiravir and Paxlovid, at-home treatments for the infected that would change the game considerably. And slowly but surely the Delta variant was being brought under control by vaccinations. So thaw the turkey, invite the family for a long-postponed holiday dinner, and start planning those Carnival costumes.

Not yet.

Now with Omicron, the conversation has shifted once again with alarm to what we don't know. Can the thirty-odd mutations on the variant's spike protein evade established immune responses provoked by previous infections or by vaccinations? That is, can people who have survived a previous COVID infection or received the three shots of vaccine still get it? The answer appears to be yes. In fact, 80 percent those of who test positive have been vaccinated. Is the infection more transmissible? Most definitely yes, much like the common cold, measles, or the flu. You might call this variant of the coronavirus "flurona." And is the infection more deadly than that caused by other variants? Apparently not, and in most cases it presents as a nagging upper-respiratory discomfort or as asymptomatic. Yet can the sniffling or asymptomatic young spread the virus to more vulnerable folk, that is, we vaccinated older people with underlying conditions?

Yes.

So this past Christmas has been marked not only by those standing in airport queues to join in joyous family reunions, but also by the interminable lines of those waiting to be tested before they even board their often canceled flights. People don't want to arrive with sacks of wrapped gifts only to mortally endanger their parents and grandparents.

The virus seems to be getting as tired of us as we are of it. Widely contagious but of a low fatality rate, Omicron now appears to be everywhere at once but nowhere really at all, a promiscuous femme fatale who comes on to everyone but usually hoofs it home to her tomb alone. Nationwide, positive test results are up 98 percent. For the first time I hear of these positive test results among people I know: the hostess of a Christmas party I attend in the Marigny calls two days later to tell me that the two waiters from the Napoleon House whom I met there tested positive. Last month my neighbor and his wife went on a foolhardy Caribbean cruise, and now he tells me that his wife has tested positive three times in a row, yet he has tested negative as many times. They continue to sleep together as man and wife, but neither have any symptoms.

Which brings us to the overwhelming question: What do these tests mean, and how reliable are they?

The pharmacies are out of take-home test kits, and today those worried about a January surge line up for hours in their cars to be tested. Unfortunately, by midmorning many sites are out of tests, even as cars idle for six blocks waiting their turns.

The quarantine period after a positive result has been halved or the country would grind to a halt due to staffing shortages. A massive wave of testing has caused many restaurants again to close because of infected staff; sports games are canceled after players with positive results are put in quarantine; thousands of flights are canceled as airline workers are housebound; and at the last minute the curtains go down on Broadway shows. Not only do the stars test positive, but also their understudies.

Everyone seems to have a date with Omicron. I'll bet that vixen even has paid a visit to the most protected person in the world, Queen Elizabeth II, secluded in Windsor Castle.

Except for treating the unvaccinated, including many young children, ICU's are not yet overwhelmed with patients infected with Omicron. In spite of the five and a half million people worldwide who have died of the virus, both in Europe and in this country the incidence of hospital deaths of those on ventilators has declined. Yet where do these variants comes from? A Beijing epidemiologist, Wenfeng Qian, recently reported in the *Journal of Genetics and Genomics* that the Omicron variant first developed in mice before infecting humans. And what is the most common lab animal used in virology experimentation?

You guessed it. Mice.

Last year in rigorously locked-down Hong Kong, the Delta variant infection arrived from the Netherlands by way of pet shop hamsters, another animal commonly used in virology investigations. And closer to home, researchers at the Tulane National Primate Research Center across Lake Pontchartrain in Covington, Louisiana, have been infecting rhesus macaques with the coronavirus to study how COVID-19 causes infertility and impotence in the genitals of male monkeys. To the great alarm of North Shore residents, during the past two decades many of these experimental lab monkeys have escaped from the primate laboratory, in one instance more than fifty at a time.

Mice, hamsters, and now, too close to home, monkeys on the North Shore. Are these variants of the SARS virus mutating inside of lab animals during scientific studies, then accidentally spilling over into the human population? "By moving between species," the

BBC News reports, "the virus can mutate and evolve into a new pathogen, which could explain how COVID-19 emerged." I'm willing to "follow the science," as we've been encouraged to do during this pandemic, as long as it doesn't lead us to lab experiments inside of Dr. Frankenstein's castle. Studying the statistics, I ponder these horror-movie possibilities while planning my réveillon gumbo dinner before Midnight Mass for Christmas Eve, the traditional Creole event I skipped last year. This year we'll be eight, and most guests I invite are skittish, confirming at the last minute. Making my list and checking it twice, I'm made to feel like a draconian Santa: *you will eat gumbo at my house and be merry, damn it!* An air purifier hums in a corner, muffled by Handel's *Messiah* cranked up loud. Our champagne glasses clink in toasts over the bûche de Noël. The Latin Mass I attend at St. Patrick's after the réveillon lasts for two hours, a Gregorian aerobics workout of repeated standing, kneeling, and sitting. I probably reek of gumbo crabs and turkey stock to those around me, but it's with a fortifying nostalgia that I take in the musky scent of frankincense wafting from the censors swung by processions of altar boys. After the past two years immersed in the pandemic panic around me, that I'm still able to stand and smell the incense on Christmas morning leaves me feeling grateful and awash in sentiment.

I share in Communion kneeling at the altar, "taking it on the tongue," as my painter cousin calls it, rather than receiving the Host in opened hands. That was a sanitary precaution initiated in the nervous eighties during the AIDS epidemic, which I also survived.

Somewhere at this moment in the packed church is probably my predetermined date with Omicron. Standing unmasked, elbow to elbow with fellow worshippers, and then sticking out my tongue on which the priest places the wafer, I cut loose months of stored up fear, anger, and denial to put my fate in God's hands. As if it has ever been anywhere else.

Five days later, in spite of this disturbing spike in an ongoing pandemic I can no longer even pretend to understand, I'm still here. As far as our Christmas Eve date was concerned, Omicron, that mousey floozy, seems to have gone home alone. And so did I.

18

Ever since March of 2020, when the coronavirus lockdown began, murders of jet black crows have been winging over New Orleans. Or perhaps I just noticed them for the first time from my third-story balcony in the Luling Mansion, but now they've followed me here to the Marigny, where looming flocks of them cross the sky, their caws echoing inside the courtyard. I wonder if they could be the carrion crows common in Europe, often believed to be messengers of death. Does this bird, known as the *corvus corone* or the crown crow, bear any relation to that other crown besieging us, the coronavirus? They both seemed to appear at the same moment. Friends all over the city report their appearance during the past couple of years, and some have recently been horrified by how the crows swoop down to attack the plastic bags of garbage left rotting on sidewalks. Trash collection has been unreliable since Hurricane Ida, and these omnivorous scavengers often appear like rats nose-diving from the sky.

Every time I sit at my glass-topped table in the courtyard, they swoop overhead, ominous as the setting for a Greek tragedy, particularly at this neurotic moment in New Orleans. However many people now test positive for the virus, ever since the optimistic parade statistics were tabulated from the Krewe of Boo, a bash-up of a Carnival season is being planned. As in Mann's *Death in Venice*, tourism has won out over public health precautions. Meanwhile, to keep up appearances, a third indoor face mask mandate has just gone into effect in Orleans Parish, and vaccinations passports are required for entering restaurants, bars, gyms, and music venues. During Mardi Gras, this will require some complicated costume adjustments, with vaccination certificates stashed in G-strings and under wigs.

Caw. Caw. Caw.

In spite of the menacing crows overhead, this afternoon has the timing of a Marx Brothers movie, a madcap scenario of positive test results. I'm seated under the flowering belladonna tree, on the phone with my niece in California, due at any moment to give birth to her second child. She confesses that both she and her husband had upper-respiratory symptoms this past Christmas, after visiting with her brother-in-law, who later tested positive for the coronavirus. Yet she still resists being vaccinated because of her pregnancy. Arguing with her won't help, so the furious imp of the perverse that has haunted me during the pandemic grows legs tall enough to look others face-to-face in the eyes with compassion.

"I also started sneezing my head off last month," I assure her, telling her that along with several friends, for a week I walked around sniffling with a handkerchief in my hand. "Probably something I picked up at Midnight Mass." Although even in winter I seldom get head colds, and hardly ever the flu, I saw no reason to scramble around looking for a coronavirus test. I knew my symptoms would pass, as they did, certain that I didn't need to consult a doctor, much less be hospitalized. I imagined that while taking it on the tongue at the altar, I'd finally kept my inevitable date with Omicron. *Agnus Dei, qui tollis peccata mundi, miserere nobis.*

"Yet I'm concerned about your two-year-old and the new baby," I tell my niece. "Young children are filling up the ICUs. Maybe you should consider being vaccinated for their sake, since they can't be."

At that moment a neighbor rushes out his back door into the courtyard, bellowing something about a positive test. I put down the phone while he explains that his wife's son, a nurse, just tested positive for the virus, and now the neighbor has to drive his wife to Thibodaux to care for her two premature grandbabies, twins who spent their first three months in incubators.

Then, after blowing my nose, I'm back on the phone with my niece, talking about testing, babies, and Omicron.

My next call is from hairdresser Mickey, canceling my appointment for later this week. His coworker alerted him that she tested positive, so he's been forced to close his shop for a week. Still worried about his business remaining open, the real ache is in his pocketbook.

Then I phone Marsha, my artist friend in Huntsville, Alabama. Although she just tested positive, she's been up on a ladder painting the walls of her new studio. "Just sneezing and a scratchy throat," she complains. I advise her to go to bed and sleep for twelve hours, which seems to cure my symptoms, whether of a cold, flu, or Omicron.

One out of every five people in Louisiana test positive, and that's only among the reported cases, not including at-home results. After the dire scenarios from last spring of hospital wards packed with elderly patients wheezing on respirators, we're now focusing on sneezing, babies, and the often bizarre symptoms of those with compromised immune systems. Gone are the early preventive obligations of handsanitizer stations and social distancing, although the tables with squirt bottles and the six-foot floor markings remain.

Now the new national mania is testing.

Currently the "white coats," as government officials call the medical scientists studying the coronoavirus, continue to ask the "old questions" with which they've become so comfortable, expecting what Samuel Beckett's senile character Hamm in *Endgame* calls the "old answers," the ones he relishes so much: "There's nothing like them!" The old questions involve how to end the pandemic and win the war against COVID, surges in infections taking on the urgency of air-raid sirens that warn of bombing raids. Much like during any wartime scenario, we stand in lines for hours, show our papers, wear protective gear, follow arrows, and wait for official updates. Public health has become militarized, and we're expected to take collective combative actions for the common good, much like employees forced to pee into plastic cups to win the War on Drugs, or taking off our shoes in airport TSA lines to triumph in the War on Terror. But in spite of the good foot soldiers most of us have become, have these militarized measures helped us to eliminate drugs and terrorists? I doubt that the ninety-two thousand Americans who died of drug overdoses last year, or the desperate people of Afghanistan and the victims of domestic terrorism, would agree. Most would insist that we've lost major ground since we began these aggressive campaigns.

Military thinking provides a pivotal metaphor in medical jargon: someone is "battling cancer" or "fighting off" an infection. As rousing as this rhetoric may sound in the contexts of our own health, the victory-or-defeat model may not apply to the slippery tactics of dealing with the stealthy spread of drug addiction, terrorist attacks, or global viral infections. As of the beginning of this year, these white coats are beginning to put statistics aside to ask a shocking new question, previously unimaginable: "If we can't eradicate this virus, how can we learn to live with an endemic disease for the long haul?"

And their answers are often confusing and contradictory, because there is no definitive one.

Various mutations of the coronavirus, such as SARS, have been under study for the past twenty years. COVID-19 is only the most current of these variants. By comparison, malaria was first noted in Egypt in 1550 BC, cholera in India in the fifth century BC, and tuberculosis nine thousand years ago. Only recently do we have vaccines against these plagues that have killed millions upon millions throughout the ages, along with yellow fever, polio, and smallpox. Although there is still no vaccine to prevent HIV, effective antiviral and preventive treatments have been developed. Routine sexual practices have changed, and after millions of deaths, we've learned to live with it.

These plagues don't simply burst upon us out of the blue and then depart defeated in a retinue of carriages filled with skeletons waving farewell with black handkerchiefs, as the screen fades back to the good old days of the way our lives used to be. Much as Samuel Pepys noted in his diary documenting the bubonic plague in London, they spike during what Anthony Fauci terms "sawtooth" outbreaks: "It goes up and then it looks like it comes down, but then it goes back up again." All of these plagues arrived in various parts of the world, causing prolonged national emergencies such as our present one, characterized by fear, panic, anger, and systemic breakdowns, along with the heroic devotion of caregivers. Then these pandemics subsided, only to reappear in other parts of the world, often centuries later, carried by ships, overland trade, wars, and colonialism, ready to ripen again in new populations unprotected by any immunological memory of the disease.

This was before vaccines were developed over the centuries to largely eradicate them, yet also before the massive air travel throughout a world now instantaneously interconnected. So we're not yet prepared for the old question of "when will this scourge be over?" to be put to rest by an old answer of "as soon as everyone in this country is vaccinated." What about the other countries in our hive-like globe? Fauci claims that "the impact on society should not be measured by how many people are blowing their noses but by how many people are really getting sick." The length of the requisite quarantine after a positive test result keeps changing, now down from ten days to five. This is a matter of great debate among the white coats. Almost half of those hospital patients who test positive for COVID are admitted for other conditions, and no distinction is made between those patients who happen to be hospitalized *with* COVID and those exclusively admitted *for* COVID. The incidental cases are counted in the spiking infection statistics. A lot of energy is wasted testing asymptomatic people. A conservative estimate now is that 40 percent of those Americans who have been tested at one point registered a positive result, not counting the at-home tests.

Yet, another complete lockdown would be disastrous. What are we to do while a third of the workforce sits alone at home, sniffling?

Even when the state of emergency disappears, many are convinced that the disease will again mutate but remain with us. For instance, forty years after the first AIDS deaths in this country, the chief epicenters of the epidemic are no longer among gay men in San Francisco and New York but among heterosexual Black women in Washington, DC, and Florida. As with HIV, what we're not sure about is whether here, there, or everywhere, the coronavirus will menace us for years, decades, or even centuries into the future, which form it may take, and to whom it will prove fatal.

This has become a particularly sobering time for us older folks considering our approaching mortality and a suffocating period for the young, impatient to celebrate their fleeting immortality. Yet old or young, at this point we must assume that the virus will be with us for the rest of our lives.

And whenever you happen to be reading these words, that moment begins right now.

Whether you're destined to die from the pandemic or not, I hope you have a guitar on which to play these mournful, jarring, and vacillating riffs that we've been listening to for the past two years. While crows scavenge above, cotton swabs are jammed up our noses, and the fabric of trade and human relations seems to be unraveling, writing this book has become mine.

Caw. Caw. Caw.

Once again, even as the carrion crows swoop overhead, I turn on a CD of Paco de Lucía's flamenco guitar and pour myself a glass of Rioja. Like the ebony clock in the cloistered purple and scarlet chambers of Poe's "The Masque of the Red Death," the Landry clock chimes on the marble mantel, much as it did on another block of Bourbon Street during the yellow fever outbreaks of the late nineteenth century. I'm a descendant of those few Creole siblings who happened to survive: the bachelor Louis who, like his father Numa, became a banker in the French Quarter; Tante Blanche, who married into a wine-dealing Catalan family, the Gelpis; and my own grande Mémère, Alice Glaudot, with whom I sat playing checkers at five years old in our Seventh Ward shotgun. In her mideighties, with a disheveled topknot of white hair, I had to shout into her one good ear when dinner was ready.

These family members never told this little boy about the plague they lived through or about the coffins of their four brothers and sisters that they accompanied to St. Louis Cemetery Number Two, where they were first buried. And I don't think the restless child I was at the time would have understood, nor will my newly born grand-niece and namesake grandnephew in California want to hear about the coronavirus epidemic of the early 2020s, much less about the polio and AIDS of my own childhood and younger years. This is how we survive through the generations, not only with the stories we pass down but by those we choose not to tell. Staring through a darkening screen door abuzz with mosquitoes as early evening approaches, we clutch a small hand inside our own gnarled fingers, silent about what we had to endure to still be here.

Mardi Gras Intermezzo

Dust in the Air

Dust in the air suspended
Marks the place where a story ended.
—T. S. Eliot, "Little Gidding"

On the Friday before Mardi Gras, standing at the corner of Common Street and St. Charles Avenue watching the Krewe of Hermes parade, I've burst out crying and am not sure why.

Maybe it's because as a child my family always took me to see Hermes, a parade in which an uncle rode the floats, as my Irish grandmother did in the Krewe of Iris. At age ten, I was a page in the Hermes ball. This is one of the most traditional and spectacularly designed parades during the Carnival season and the first one I've witnessed during the past two years. Or perhaps the tears flow because the pandemic, for the moment, seems to have abated. As I stand here alone, everyone around me is having fun with a vengeance: laughing, toasting, yelling for throws, and bouncing shoulder to shoulder to the infectious rhythm of the brass band marching behind the float. To say the least, nobody is socially distancing or wearing a face mask.

Whatever the reason, the flowered float titled "The Angel Brings the Book of Sophocles" makes me blink back tears.

A girl standing next to me, no more than ten years old, looks up to study this peculiar older gentleman not jigging in place or scrambling for throws, tears running down his cheeks from under his glasses. And with a beguiling smile she reaches up to hand me three of her prized gold Hermes necklaces. Choking back sobs, I thank her then drape them around my neck, as if the angel himself had handed me the book of Sophocles in which pestilence has been vanquished from plague-besieged Thebes.

Is this how our own Sophocles-like tragedy is supposed to end?

When watching Orpheus, the parade I see the next Monday, and during the tropical warmth of Mardi Gras afternoon, while perched on a Royal Street balcony dressed as the Prince of Pearls to observe the crowds reveling below, I hold back a bit, as if waiting for the other shoe to drop. I ask myself if this Carnival season, which we need so much, represents a triumph of public health over a now-endemic virus or of the tourism industry over medical caution. I keep thinking back to the vertiginous surges and remissions of infection in the plague narratives of Boccaccio, Defoe, Pepys, and Camus, and wonder when, where, and how the curse of this pestilence might again be repeated.

At the moment, I'm neither a pessimist nor an optimist but, like most people, burned out by it all, toasted to a crisp. My initial alarm about Carnival came when Dr. Jennifer Avegno, director of the New Orleans Public Health Department, a fellow native of the city who had come down hard with unpopular face mask and vaccination certificate mandates throughout the Mardi Gras season, was named queen of the satirical Krewe du Vieux. This raucous walking krewe with mule-drawn floats parades two weeks before Mardi Gras through the French Quarter and respects no limits in their graphic sexuality and caustic skewering of local politics. Naming Dr. Avegno as the queen of a farcical parade with the theme "Vaxxed and Confused" seemed like a truce between the factions at war about the pandemic.

Until she decided not to ride in the parade because of the death threats lobbed against her.

My imagination reeled at such a grotesque scenario, one somehow so appropriate to New Orleans: if the director of Public Health had been shot dead while seated on the queen's throne of the Krewe du Vieux parade, all bets would have been off regarding this Carnival and the city's handling of the pandemic. Once again, I realized that the more dangerous problem isn't the virus but in ourselves and how we've handled it as people, a city, and a nation.

"This is what happened during the sickness," writes the Greek historian Thucydides at the end of each chapter of his *History of the Peloponnesian War*, an account of the fifth century BC war between Athens and Sparta during a pestilence that ravaged the Athenian population. "The victims of a pandemic are not only the infected, but those who suffer from the crime and demoralization that accompany it," explains W. Robert Connor in his essay, "Reading Thucydides in a Time of Pandemic," in the *American Scholar*. "Under such stress human nature shows its vicious side. . . . The Greek term, *orge*, often translated as anger or rage, includes as well a loss of the ability to restrain any number of intense emotions and drives. It implies that the Athenians were not just angry; their emotions had taken over, affecting their ability to make sound judgments. Even worse, Thucydides implies, they were not aware of what was happening to them."

Greek *orge* is the only word to describe what last month may have motivated Canadians, among the most even-tempered people on earth, to form "freedom convoys" of enraged truck drivers and their supporters to shut down Ottawa in a chaotic protest against pandemic restrictions and vaccine mandates. These horn-blaring demonstrations soon spread to Toronto, Quebec City, Calgary, and the Ambassador Bridge, the route that connects Ontario to Michigan, halting commercial trade between the two counties until President Trudeau enforced the Emergency Act for the first time in Canadian history. Weeks later, an American version of the ballistic "freedom convoys" fizzled out on the Beltway in Washington, DC.

Then Russian troops lined up along the border with Ukraine, preparing an invasion that they have since executed with unprovoked *orge* and a barbaric disregard for civilian lives. Once again, as Thucydides writes, "this is what happened during the sickness."

During this sickness, to date there have been more than six million deaths worldwide and almost a million in the United States. Yet Dr. Avegno is pleased to report that among the 146 coronavirus results reported by Carnival parade-goers who volunteered their contact information, only six tested positive. And Dr. Walensky, director of the CDC, who last fall confessed during a televised meltdown to a "feeling of ominous doom," now claims that while pandemic developments were previously profiled in the starkest terms of black-and-white—*bump elbows or die!*—we should now think of the pandemic "in shades of gray." This is precisely the "we-don't-know-but . . ." approach to medical reporting that I've been waiting for during the rollercoaster ride of the past two years. It restores my confidence in public health, whose often alarmist hyperboles sparked a state of national panic beginning in March of 2020.

In this post-Carnival season of Lent, exactly two years after this pandemic began in New Orleans, I'm still left waiting on the curb straining to see if another cavalcade, the ghastly funeral cortege of the coronavirus, has come to an end. As murders of crows continue to circle the sky, I hear a buzz among the crowd that two more viral floats soon may be on the way: the BA.2 mutation now spiking in Europe, expected to be 30 to 50 percent more contagious than the previous variant of Omicron, and a hybrid genome referred to as Deltacron, a combination of the two variants. Despite the lifting of most health restrictions in this country, there's little indication that this particular procession is finally over. As one scientist recently put it, "We're wearing rose-colored glasses instead of correcting our vision."

Through the rosy tint of the lenses I'm now wearing on this spring equinox, all I can make out in the street ahead is a cloud of dust suspended in the air.

Has the story ended?

Along with most of the world, what I'm now waiting for on this curb is the definitive appearance of what in my childhood was called the "crash truck." This was a sturdy vehicle with a crane, siren, and flashing red lights that rolled past to signal the end of a Carnival parade, a truck equipped to rescue any floats that may have broken down along the route.

Pulling this little boy out of the clamoring crowd by his shoulder, my Great-Aunt Marguerite would point to the revolving red lights. "Look, it's the crash truck," she'd say. "The parade is over."

Then she'd grab me by the hand. "It's time to go home."

March 20, 2022

Ebb Tide

*Let us comb the silent
blue shore for dark things . . .
after the devastating storm
has roared past like a train.*

—Pablo Neruda, "Pay No Attention to Me"

On May 3, 2023, the US Surgeon General, Dr. Vivek Murthy, issued an advisory about the impact of a new epidemic: one of loneliness and lack of social connection. He compared the unhealthy effects of the widespread isolation we Americans are experiencing to those of tobacco, obesity, and substance abuse, claiming this lack of personal interaction creates serious risks for heart disease, stroke, anxiety, and dementia, leading to a 60 percent increase in premature deaths. This was two days before the World Health Organization declared an end to the COVID-19 Public Health Emergency, and a week before President Biden announced that the pandemic was over in the United States.

After two and half years of lockdown, when most institutions and businesses were shuttered while we were ordered to stay home and hide under our beds, it should surprise no one that the epidemic now threatening our health is one of isolation. Of course, Dr. Murthy didn't mention the long-lasting effects of the lockdown and social distancing policies of Dr. Rochelle Walensky, former director of the Center for Disease Control—who mid-pandemic sensed an "ominous doom" on the horizon—or of retired Dr. Anthony Fauci, chief medical adviser to the president, who initiated most of the restrictive coronavirus policies.

Who would have suspected those years of hiding under our beds would lead to an ongoing epidemic of loneliness?

This is a blazingly hot summer in New Orleans, but a chill creeps down my spine every time I pass red-headed Laura's house, a block from mine in the Marigny Triangle. She was a tenured university professor of American literature, one who taught several of my books in her classes, and I treasure a few of the insightful term papers her students wrote about them. As the pandemic began, she was forced to teach her rigorous four-classes-per-semester schedule by Zoom, so for almost three years she rose at dawn to sit in front of a computer screen, never sure which students were involved in the sessions, who dropped in or out, and how to grade them. Five days a week, she was on call twelve grueling hours a day for these remote sessions, as well as student email and phone consultations, a glass of white wine always in her hand. She'd never worked so hard in her long career, she complained, and ordered her half-gallon jugs of wine by the case.

Last autumn, as she lay dying of cirrhosis of the liver in the hospice bed in her living room, she raised a bony hand to bid me goodbye during our final visit. A wide streak of gray parted her fiery hair at the scalp, a sure sign that this jazz musician's girlfriend had given up on her bon vivant French Quarter life. When I took her hand to kiss it, I thought I was bidding goodbye to the pandemic. I had little idea this was a moment of slack tide, before the outgoing ebb tide of the pandemic was to expose the extensive damage that distancing, lockdown, and widespread panic had done to us, both as individuals and as a society. Now that teachers and nurses, along with cops and ambulance workers, are resigning in droves, leaving schools, hospitals, police forces, and emergency services sorely understaffed, we're forced to confront the true cost of the pandemic in the lives of those who once served us.

It's called burnout.

Last autumn, not only Laura but nine other friends of mine were to pass away, none from the coronavirus itself but each from some destructive aspect of the extended duration of the lockdown. Their ages were from eighteen—a high school senior who, after three years of remote classes, fatefully set out to celebrate his virtual graduation from my alma mater, Benjamin Franklin—to a wheelchair-bound eighty-seven-year-old Tennessee Williams scholar who withered away in social isolation. One was a doctor, another a nurse. As the obituaries poured in, I saw a pattern. It was as if, after the pandemic began with its ensuing restrictions, everyone took a collective deep breath, determined to survive. Like a soldier approaching the front with a set jaw and clenched teeth, a willful determination took over: *I will get through this.* Then, even before the end of the national health emergency was announced this May, they finally exhaled.

They had survived.

And then they died.

Another chill crept down my spine last month when a waiter was gunned down in a drive-by shooting in front of Mandina's, the holy of holies of traditional neighborhood restaurants. The twenty-two-year-old shooter bolted out of his car, killed a waiter standing outside, and in the barrage of ensuing gunfire a bullet pierced the walls to wound a fifty-four-year-old woman from Chicago, in town for the first Friday of Jazz Fest. A security guard returned fire, but the hoodlums sped away, only to be apprehended a week later in Houston, after killing a fifteen-year-old. Mandina's is across Canal Street from Schoen & Son Funeral Home, where for generations my family's funerals have taken place. After wakes and burials we'd often gather there for a repast meal. Mourning to me has always tasted like their sherry-laced turtle soup.

New Orleans is now the murder capitol of the United States. Since 2020, the police force has been depleted by a fourth, so five hundred—approximately two-thirds—of the murderers haven't been caught, much less tried or jailed. We residents need to steel ourselves against the fever of lawlessness and violence overtaking us during this pandemic ebb tide. An automobile is stolen every hour, pistol-waving carjackings occur every day, and along entire blocks the windows of parked vehicles are shattered and the insides ransacked, even in paid parking lots and garages. Teenagers are gunning each other down in record numbers, not only on the mean back streets but at high school graduation bashes, college commencement ceremonies, birthday parties, funerals, and second lines.

After almost three years of lockdown, a widespread lack of civility bred by social isolation is evident not only in raging airline passengers expressing their *orge* or but in daily interactions on the street. Normally, when strolling past each other on the sidewalk in New Orleans, we locals exchange a greeting in recognition of passing a fellow human being. Yet now young people stride by with expressionless faces. If not staring at their cell phones, it's as if they're still wearing the pandemic masks they were raised with. One secondary school principal in Richmond, Virginia, notes that after reopening the classrooms, socialization among students posed a huge challenge.

"What does it look like when you and another student disagree?" she asked them.

These days, headlines betray their response: you pull out a gun and shoot them.

The lack of interpersonal connection has been replaced by social media and guns among many adolescents who have been on the loose for a long while, neither in school, at home, nor in any other structured environment. Even when local schools did reopen, the truancy rate has remained at 10 percent. Much like the failed public health and safety interventions of Prohibition and the War on Drugs, many of the regulations of the coronavirus pandemic have created a thriving criminal underclass that threatens the public order much more than booze or weed ever did. Yet in this case, the violence hasn't come from the profit-driven Mafia or drug cartels, which at least represented organized crime, but from something much more insidious: *unorganized crime*. Although now both alcohol and cannabis are legal, these unsupervised juveniles were ill-fated to have come of age during an era when going to school, church, playgrounds, or sporting events wasn't. And they're making the downtowns of many major American cities unlivable with a nonstop soundtrack of wailing sirens.

Except for a spray of stray bullets from this unorganized crime, I'm not particularly afraid. I don't have a car, gun, or any drugs, and evidently this septuagenarian plodding along from the grocery trailing a granny cart doesn't carry much cash. Yet the massacre at Mandina's was too intimate a call, as if it had happened in my grandmother's living room. Now nobody in this city—young or old, Black or White, tourist or resident—feels safe. While we were self-isolating and both the streets and schools were emptied, these unmoored kids were festering in gangs, stunting both their learning and social skills. Almost three years of remote education have resulted in plummeting reading and math scores among primary and secondary school students, and test results are most discouraging in the areas that were the slowest to reopen. From one end of the social spectrum to the other, their futures look bleak. As Stanford economist Eric Hanushek predicts, "this cohort of students is going to be punished throughout their lifetime."

They are a new Lost Generation.

*

On this sweltering summer solstice, get ready for a splash of cold water to the face. The sobering global mortality numbers are in, and I hope they guide us in how we deal with future pandemics. According to the W.H.O., as of June 3, 6,938,340 people worldwide died of reported cases of COVID-19. In spite of our extensive public health structures and the strict precautions taken in most states, the United States leads other countries with 1,127,152 deaths, the most in the world. This is followed only by the laissez-faire public health policies in the Brazil of pandemic-denying Jair Bolsonaro, with its 702,664 deaths, and the 531,867 mortalities in chaotic, overpopulated India, as impossible to regulate as a buzzing beehive. Surprisingly, these numbers were almost reached during the serial lockdowns in the United Kingdom, with 226,278 deaths, trailed by notoriously hygienic Germany with 174,691 fatalities, and heavily quarantined France with its 163,844 mortalities. As I suspected, the controversial herd immunity policy of unlocked-down Sweden resulted in a fraction of the mortalities elsewhere in the European Union, with only 24,471 deaths, most of them in nursing homes. Yet this was more than double the number of fatalities among Sweden's Scandinavian neighbors.

Within this country, the insular geography of strictly locked-down Hawaii guaranteed the lowest per capita number of deaths. Yet defiantly unregulated Florida (population 21.78 million) had a lower mortality rate than rigidly quarantined New York (population 19.84 million).

I wonder if any epidemiologist can make sense of these numbers as a reflection of pandemic policies.

What they do reflect is how intricately entwined these health policies have been with local and national politics, as has been the case in all of the plague literature I've cited, from Thucydides and Boccacio through Defoe and Camus. In the two worst-hit countries, both pandemic-denying Trump and Bolsonaro were narrowly defeated in hotly contested presidential elections. In what seems like a lost chapter of Defoe's *Journal of the Plague Year*, Boris Johnson was forced to resign not only as the prime minister of the United

Kingdom but from Parliament because of the "party-gate" scandal, in which that shaggy-haired Tory rascal in charge of the series of national quarantines was accused of hosting "jingle and mingle" Christmas wine parties.

In most countries, the numbers tell the story, but we'll never know the true statistics from secretive China, where the virus originated, or learn with any certainty if it was leaked from a lab or spread from a live food market. Yet China's draconian "Zero COVID" policies were the most spectacular failure in the world, resulting in the exact opposite of its intended goals. Much like during the Cultural Revolution, when the political correctness of every citizen's "Mao Zedong Thought" was routinely challenged, pandemic policy became an ideological campaign to tighten the government's control over people's daily lives. Everybody was tested daily for COVID, proof of negative results was required to take the subway or enter a workplace, and those testing positive were forced into weeklong quarantines in squalid barracks or welded inside their homes. All parks and public gathering places were barricaded and policed, and even casual contact with an infected person the previous day could justify a long confinement.

In November of last year, the normally compliant Chinese finally exploded, thronging the streets during riotous protests in Beijing, Shanghai, and throughout Guangzhou province. This was the first public challenge to the totalitarian control of the Communist party since the massacre at Tiananmen Square in 1989, five years after I left my university teaching position in China. Even then, face masks were as much a part of Chinese life as chopsticks, and Beijing was the first place I ever wore one, not to avoid viral contagion but simply to bicycle through the oppressive pollution. That post-Maoist era of Deng Xiaoping and his "Opening to the West" was when the Chinese made a tacit pact with their government, surrendering their personal freedom in return for prosperity.

Since then, impoverished feudal China has disappeared. Skyscrapers have risen and factories flourished.

Yet during the pandemic years, with the factories shuttered and people imprisoned inside their cement high-rise apartments, they had neither freedom nor prosperity. All international travel was banned, and anyone entering China had to endure a monthlong quarantine. Threatened by a popular uprising for the first time in decades, President Xi Jinping abruptly suspended "Zero COVID" restrictions, and life returned to normal.

Almost.

Yet with little herd immunity and spotty inoculations with a less effective vaccine, the virus surged, especially among the elderly. Millions sickened, and hundreds of thousands died. Hospitals overflowed with the infected and crematoriums with corpses. The totalitarian grip on the people that pandemic policies were meant to enforce backfired, breeding distrust, simmering rebellion, an exodus of immigrants, and probably—we'll never know for sure—the worst toll the coronavirus has exacted on any population.

In *The Plague*, Camus chose well in using emergency medical policy as a metaphor for Nazi-occupied France. Like Hitler's invaders, Camus's doctors insisted to the resistant population that the controls were for their own good. With the hindsight now offered during this ebb tide, what has happened in China and the rest of the world should warn us to be as wary of a pandemic's politics as of its germs.

A chill also runs down my spine every time I pass the shuttered hair salon on Toulouse Street of that expansive Cajun, Mickey. He fought tooth and nail to keep his business running during the pandemic years, undergoing routine inspections and observing to the letter-of-the-law all city and federal health restrictions. I remember waiting for a haircut outside on the street in the sweltering heat until his previous client had left, observing the occupancy limit, and having my sideburns shaved while wearing a face mask, no easy maneuver. Early last year his phone line was disconnected, and then I learned from another hair dresser at his shop that he'd developed a debilitating case of long COVID. The next time I walked by, the windows were dark, and the salon was gone. Along with visits to my deceased neighbor Laura, Mickey's haircuts were among the few social contacts I maintained during the pandemic years.

I'm not sure if hairdresser Mickey's "essential business," which remained open during most of the lockdown, received any of the relief assistance offered by the federal government to aid failing and closed commercial enterprises. If so, considering how hard he worked, he deserved it, unlike the looted 280 billion dollars scammed from three huge federal relief programs launched during the initial surges of the pandemic, meant to help the unemployed as well as closed businesses. Much like Trump's blustering responses to other complex problems, such as his "build the wall" solution to the immigration crisis at the southern border, the president sought to rid the country of the virus by throwing wads of money at it in every imaginable direction. But it didn't work. The *New York Times* has called this heist the "greatest grift in U.S. history," stolen from what was meant to be the largest rescue package our economy has ever undertaken, including Roosevelt's Works Progress Administration during the Depression, which did manage to catch another economy in free fall. This early stampede of bogus online applications and swindled payouts no doubt has contributed to the runaway inflation we've suffered since the recovery, as well as to the ballooning national debt.

I assume that my health club did receive legitimate business rescue funds from the government. Its locker rooms, swimming pool, saunas, and steam rooms were undoubtedly hotbeds of contagion during most of the pandemic, so along with gyms nationwide, it was shut down for almost two years. Last summer it returned to full service, and I'm pleased to have taken up my swimming and steaming routines again. Yet I notice that since the reopening, a pandemic hangover has dramatically changed the atmosphere of this historic French Quarter athletic club, founded in 1872. Now black-framed placards of numbered rules and regulations clutter its walls, and although I've never put on my reading glasses to study them, they make the club feel as uptight as a Mormon penal colony. By the way, this is the same club that Tennessee Williams frequented and where he set his racy short story "One Armed Masseuse."

After opening all of its facilities, social distancing signs and handsanitizer stations were positioned everywhere, and as a member for almost twenty-five years, I soon noticed that the club's once relaxing conviviality had changed for the worst, as if overseen by the American Taliban. Men now have to shower and dry ourselves behind cheesy plastic curtains inside the antique marble stalls, the only place where nudity is permitted. Just last month members were emailed "A Few Gym Etiquette Tips to Remember," which included this phobic advisory: "Please do not stare at others while working out, even through mirrors. If you can see them, they can see you."

During various historical eras this country has been a bleached blond of irrepressible fun—most recently in the twenties, sixties, and nineties, from Mae West to Harlow, Marilyn to Janis Joplin, then on to Madonna. But once again its Puritan roots are showing, and poor Mickey the hairdresser is no longer around to highlight them. Dr. Murthy, I'm afraid we'll be living with your loneliness epidemic far longer than Dr. Fauci's coronavirus pandemic. We've become accustomed to hiding under the beds of our digital self-incarcerations, first from the virus and now from the people who once transmitted it.

Remember: *If you can see them, they can see you.*

Of course, here in New Orleans, the brothel again is wide open, since mass tourism is the only industry we have. During the innumerable conventions, festivals, holiday weekends, bachelor and bachelorette parties, and destination weddings, downtown sidewalks are packed with tourists cavorting in gangs of go-cup-sloshing revelers. They're letting their post-pandemic hair down to engage in long-prohibited revenge travel, and New Orleans architecture, music, and culture are merely atmospheric backdrops for their indulgent selfies. Burgeoning Airbnbs have become the crack cocaine of real estate, driving longtime residents out of their traditional neighborhoods. City politics are as corrupt, scandalous, and inept as ever, but with no high-sounding gobbledygook of well-meaning health policy to lend gravitas to the contentious fray.

Yet New Orleans as a brand isn't what I'm considering, but the city as a place, the neighborhoods and daily culture in which we residents live.

We local survivors are bursting with the desire to go somewhere and do something, even if we've forgotten how to be with each other. Last week I went with friends to see a mediocre play, but we were eager to congratulate ourselves: "This is the first time I've been to the theater in three years!" we each said in head-bobbing unison. Or to a movie. Or to eat indoors at a restaurant. Or to sit in a bar. Or go to a book signing. On first seeing each other, our hugs are hesitant, like that peck of a kiss after a first date.

Yet no matter how awkward as it may now feel, this is life as we remember it.

The transition was easier for some of us than others. I never suffered any symptoms of the virus nor was I ever tested, and what writer isn't committed to long stretches of solitude? It was much harder for others, who underwent debilitating contagions or lost loved ones to the disease. It was endurable for those of us who continued some facsimile of our former lives than for those who lost everything—businesses, professions, homes, family members, or years of formative education. Like the memories of my friends Laura the professor and Mickey the hairdresser, both indirect victims, the pandemic losses will echo throughout our entire lives.

But now, as after a war, we want more, to shrug off our "battle fatigue," currently diagnosed as post-traumatic stress disorder. After the militarization, polarization, and monetization of a worldwide pandemic, we want to return unmasked and unfettered to what we remember as our civilian lives, expecting less from politics and more from daily living.

"I think there is going to be a vast hunger for life after all this death—and for light after this eclipse," Tennessee Williams wrote to William Saroyan in November of 1941, after the attack on Pearl Harbor, foreseeing both the bleakness of the war years ahead as well as the post-war boom. "People will want to read, see, feel the living truth and they will revolt against the sing-song Mother Goose book of lies being fed to them."

August 1, 2023

ACKNOWLEDGMENTS

An excerpt from the Prologue and Part I of this book was previously published in the Spring 2022 issue of the *Xavier Review* (Volume 42. Issue 1); "My First Attempted Coup d'État," a segment from Part III, appeared in the Fulbright Association Newsletter, July 23, 2021.

I would like to acknowledge with deep gratitude the use on the front cover of artist Marsha Ercegovic's *The House of Usher*, a painting inspired by the Luling Mansion in New Orleans. And I offer my appreciation to the artist Kathleen Grieshaber for collaborating with me on the cover design of this book, including her graphic of the menacing crow motif. At UL Press, I thank production manager Mary Karnath Duhé for her expert technical assistance in realizing the cover, as well as the editor, Devon Lord, for her meticulous research and attention to detail in editing the manuscript. I also extend many thanks to Francesca Lafarouche for the author photo, to Ulysses D'Aquila for his helpful editorial suggestions during the writing process, and to the friends and neighbors who supported my efforts and helped me to endure through these challenging pandemic years along with its lingering aftermath. Nobody survives times like these on their own. We did it together.

ABOUT THE AUTHOR

JAMES NOLAN, a fifth-generation New Orleans native, is a widely published writer, poet, and translator. His latest book is *Nasty Water: Collected New Orleans Poems* (University of Louisiana at Lafayette Press, 2018), and his recent *Flight Risk: Memoirs of a New Orleans Bad Boy* (University Press of Mississippi) won the 2018 Next-Generation Indie Book Award for Best Memoir. His fiction includes *You Don't Know Me: New and Selected Stories* (winner of the 2015 Independent Publishers Gold Medal in Southern Fiction), the novel *Higher Ground* (awarded a Faulkner/Wisdom Gold Medal), and *Perpetual Care: Stories*. Other poetry collections are *Why I Live in the Forest* and *What Moves Is Not the Wind*, together with *Drunk on Salt*. His translations from the Spanish include Pablo Neruda's *Stones of the Sky* and *If Only for a Moment (I'll Never Be Young Again): Selected Poems of Jaime Gil de Biedma*. He has received an N.E.A. grant as well as a Javits and two Fulbright fellowships, and taught at universities in San Francisco, Barcelona, Madrid, Beijing, and Florida, as well as at Tulane and Loyola in New Orleans, where he now lives.